WARFARE

WARFARE

Winning the Spiritual Battle

TONY EVANS

MOODY PUBLISHERS
CHICAGO

Edited by Kevin P. Emmert
Interior design: Ragont Design
Cover design: Thinkpen Design
Cover photo of night sky copyright [copyright symbol here] 2018 by Estremo/Shutterstock (121925236). All rights reserved.

Library of Congress Cataloging-in-Publication Data

Names: Evans, Tony, 1949- author. | Evans, Tony, 1949- Battle is the Lord's.
Title: Warfare : winning the spiritual battle / Tony Evans.
Description: Chicago : Moody Publishers, 2018. | "This work is a condensed version of The Battle Is the Lord's."
Identifiers: LCCN 2018025686 (print) | LCCN 2018032095 (ebook) | ISBN 9780802496638 (ebook) | ISBN 9780802418173
Subjects: LCSH: Spiritual warfare.
Classification: LCC BV4509.5 (ebook) | LCC BV4509.5 .E8337 2018 (print) | DDC 235/.4--dc23
LC record available at https://lccn.loc.gov/2018025686

We hope you enjoy this book from Moody Publishers. Our goal is to provide high-quality, thought-provoking books and products that connect truth to your real needs and challenges. For more information on other books and products written and produced from a biblical perspective, go to www.moodypublishers.com or write to:

Moody Publishers
820 N. LaSalle Boulevard
Chicago, IL 60610

3 5 7 9 10 8 6 4 2

Printed in the United States of America

Contents

Introduction

Days after the tragedy of 9/11 struck our nation's soul, members of the Special Forces known as the Green Beret were asked to pack their bags, leave their families, and head straight into the heart of warfare. While each of us back home struggled to come to grips with the devastation that came about so suddenly, these men set out to do something about it.

They flew there with one goal in mind: stop the enemy before the enemy could make another attack on innocent lives.

The Special Forces knew that if they could get to the root of the attack in a limited amount of time, they could win the immediate war of protecting citizens on America's soil. They could protect individuals, families, churches, and communities, but only by letting go of what they once knew concerning conventional warfare and by embracing a strategy that would work.

One man, Mark Nutsch, was chosen to lead the twelve men into battle. Despite having no combat experience, his confidence and ability to think outside of normative approaches during the vetting process won him the assignment. Little did the military leaders know at the time of choosing him that Mark's experience growing up on his family's ranch, working as a ranch hand in college, and riding horses in rodeos would be one of his greatest assets.

After all, this wasn't a war fought with militaries lined up and facing each other on opposite sides. Nor was it even fought in the trenches. Rather, to excel in this war, combatants would need to battle the elements, ride horses over rough and dangerous terrain, and outwit their opponents who knew the landscape like the back of their own hands.

To win this battle, Mark and his team of eleven other brave men would have to fight according to the rules of the enemy themselves.

Their campaign was supposed to take six weeks, but due to weather, they sought to complete it in three. It was supposed to take multiple teams of Green Beret, but due to the elements, topography, and lack of entrance points, they were given only one team of twelve men. It was supposed to rack up a high level of casualties on the American side due to the risks involved, but they walked away with none.

Because these men chose to adapt to the environment and allies surrounding them and work within the strategies at hand, they accomplished what few, if any, thought they could. On horseback, they battled tanks and troops armed with missiles.

And won.

Maybe it was Mark's lack of previous combat experience that opened him up to adapting his strategy to the battle at hand more so than someone else possibly could have. We'll never know for sure. But one thing we do know is that it was his willingness to set aside conventional approaches that allowed him to approach this battle unlike any other that had been fought in the history of our nation.

It also allowed him to lead his team of twelve into the quickest, most decisive victory in the history of our nation.

Two thousand years ago, another team of twelve followed another unconventional leader. He didn't ride a horse; He rode a donkey. His battle didn't last three weeks, but three days. He didn't fight for a nation; He fought for a kingdom.

And won.

In doing so, He secured for each of us the victory that is ours to claim.

Yet only as we are willing to follow Him by laying down our own logic, perspective, approach, and understanding of how to fight this war will we discover the fullness and effects of that victory in every area of our lives. It is in following Christ as our Captain that we can win this war. It is in studying His battle plan that we can discover how to carry out our own. It is in conforming our hearts and transforming our minds to His that we will gain the strategic insights we need to live out the victory He has already secured for us.

See, this battle is unlike any other. This battle has already been decided. The outcome has already been secured. Jesus Christ gained the victory through His death, burial, and resurrection. But in order for us to experience the manifestation of that victory in our own lives, we need to learn how to maneuver through the mines left behind from an enemy still bent on making our lives miserable along the way.

It's true that many Christians don't even know they're at war. Others, however, can see clearly the results of the battle in their lives, because they have become casualties of spiritual warfare. Some suffer emotional wounds from spiritual warfare. They are discouraged, depressed, downtrodden, and defeated. Others have taken fatal blows to their marriage or family. Divorce, conflict, and abuse are some of the battle scars they bear. Still others have been morally wounded in the battle. They cannot control their passions and make poor moral choices. For some Christians, the wounds have been inflicted on their finances. They are losing the financial battle because they are losing the spiritual one.

I could list more casualties, but I assume you get the idea. Since we all are at war, and since there is so much at stake both here in history and in eternity, we had better learn what spiritual warfare is about and how we can fight successfully.

THE NATURE OF THE BATTLE

The essence of the war we're talking about is spiritual. Because this warfare is first and foremost spiritual and not physical, the degree to which you and I will be successful is the degree to which we are prepared to understand and fight this battle on a spiritual level. While waged in the invisible, spiritual realm, spiritual warfare is manifested in the visible, physical realm. In other words, spiritual warfare is a battle between invisible, angelic forces that affects you and me. You and I can't see the cause of the war, but we see the effects—the kinds of problems I mentioned above—all the time, day in and day out.

It's hard enough to fight an enemy you can see. It's much

harder to fight someone you can't see. Everything you do in the visible, physical realm is caused, provoked, or at least influenced by something in the invisible, spiritual realm. Your five senses are not the limit of reality, and until we address the spiritual root of a problem, we will never fix the physical effects of that problem.

Not only are your physical senses limited, but they often provide little help in spiritual warfare. This means that if you are going to wage successful spiritual battle, you need a "sixth sense"—a keen awareness of the spiritual realm. In order to understand spiritual warfare, we have to address it through the lens of the spirit, with the help of the Holy Spirit.

THE LOCATION OF THE BATTLE

Where in the universe is this great battle called spiritual warfare being fought? Paul tells us it is "in the heavenly places" (Eph. 6:12), which means the spiritual realm. In the Bible, the word heaven describes three levels of existence (see 2 Cor. 12:2). The first heaven is the atmosphere that surrounds the earth, the environment in which we live. The second heaven is what we commonly refer to as outer space, the stellar heavens where the stars and planets exist. This is also a realm in which angels operate, because in the Bible, angels are called stars (Job 38:7). When you see the stars at night, they should remind you of spiritual beings called angels and the reality of the warfare we are engaged in. The third heaven is the throne room of God, the place we normally think of when we hear the word heaven. It is about this heaven that the Bible has the most to say. In fact, the third heaven is an incredibly busy place because it is the control center of the universe.

In the book of Ephesians alone, we find numerous references to heavenly places in addition to that in 6:12. Understanding these passages helps us know how to tap into the heavenly places and thus wage victorious spiritual warfare.

Ephesians 1:3 says, "Blessed be the God and Father of our Lord Jesus Christ, who has blessed us with every spiritual blessing in the heavenly places in Christ." This verse tells us that God resides in the heavenly places, and so do all of our spiritual blessings. This is important because if you are engaged in a spiritual battle and need help to win, the help you need is with God the Father, who is in the heavenly places. But if you don't know how to access heavenly places, you won't know how to access the heavenly help you need to win the battle in earthly places.

You may be thinking, *But Tony, I'm facing Satan here on earth.* Yes, but your blessings are in heaven. So unless you learn how to open your arsenal of spiritual weapons in the heavenly places so you can use them down here, you'll be a casualty of the war.

According to Ephesians 1:20, when God the Father raised Jesus Christ from the dead, He seated His Son "at His right hand in the heavenly places." Not only are the Father and your blessings in heavenly places, but so is Jesus Christ. So if you need Christ's help in earthly places, you'd better know where He is hanging out and how to obtain His help in your warfare.

But it gets even better: God also "raised *us* up with [Christ], and seated us with Him in the heavenly places" (2:6, emphasis added). You and I as believers are also in heavenly places. Paul is telling us that when you accepted Christ, you were transported to another sphere. Even though your body is limited to earth, your spirit that should be controlling your body is operating in a wholly different realm.

Few Christians understand that. The most real part of our existence is what happens in our spiritual lives, not what happens in our bodies. We are residents of heaven—in our spirits now and someday in our bodies, too. Once you understand how the heavenly sphere operates, you can begin changing what happens on earth.

What else is in heavenly places? According to Ephesians 3:10, spiritual rulers and authorities are there. These are angels. Why is this important from the standpoint of spiritual warfare? Because it takes an angel to beat an angel, and 6:12 tells us that Satan and his demons are also "in the heavenly places."

OUR RESOURCES FOR THE BATTLE

All this means that if your problem originates in the heavenly places, then you need a solution that originates in the heavenly places as well. Most of us are vaguely aware of angels because they're not part of our physical world. But we need to understand that the angels of God and the demons of hell are the warriors in the cosmic battle between God and Satan.

When you hear believers say they are being attacked by the devil, they probably mean they are being harassed by his foot soldiers. Satan is a limited being, just like any other created being. He is not present everywhere, all-knowing, or all-powerful. Satan is not God, but he has a whole host of evil angels called demons he can use for spiritual attacks. Anything that hell can bring against you results from satanic activity in the same realm in which God operates, called the heavenly places.

You and I are no match for the power and deceptiveness of Satan and his army. We need the power of God to neutralize and eventually overcome Satan's attacks against us. We can be thankful that God has established His throne in heavenly places, pitting His kingdom against the kingdom of darkness. The kingdom of darkness has its own king, Satan, and he wants to be in charge of the universe. Yet when it comes to the universe, there's no question that God's kingdom and His King, Jesus Christ, are firmly in charge. And Jesus' eternal victory is already assured. Still, God has allowed us to choose in our individual lives who will rule over us.

THE REASON FOR THE BATTLE

Revelation 12 depicts a day when the invisible warfare in the heavenly places will break out in a very visible form. Verse 7 shows us who the enemy is in this conflict: "And there was war in heaven, Michael and his angels waging war with the dragon. The dragon and his angels waged war." The archangel Michael and the holy angels are fighting Satan and the angels who rebelled with him. The battle is angelic, but they are fighting over the earth. Thus, the war in heaven directly affects what is happening on earth.

We are in the midst of an angelic conflict, a satanic rebellion, in which Satan is seeking to bring this whole world under his rule. That means when you were born into the kingdom of God, you were born into a war. You were born a warrior. You are surrounded by a spiritual enemy, but the battle is not for land or anything physical. This cosmic battle is for *glory*. The issue is: Who is going to get the glory in this universe? Who is going to be worshiped? Who will have notoriety? Who will get to call the shots?

Satan has essentially said to God, "You cannot have all the glory in creation. I want some of the glory for myself."

God's response? "My glory I will not give to another" (Isa. 48:11).

Of course that answer didn't sit well with Satan, so he set about to steal what was not rightfully his—glory. The battle is for glory. Understanding that is half the fight. That's why Paul told us, "Whatever you do, do all to the glory of God" (1 Cor. 10:31; see also Col. 3:23).

Glory—it's what the battle is all about.

1

The Origins of Our Battle

Touring Israel with others is one of my favorite activities. Every so often, our national radio broadcast ministry, *The Urban Alternative*, organizes a group to visit with us, and I spend time teaching through the biblical scenarios that took place at various sites. Israel is truly a miraculous, breathtaking place. I can also honestly say I've never felt safer than those times when I was in the Holy Land. That statement may surprise you. After all, we witness horrendous bombings, rumors of wars, and great conflict on news outlets concerning this region. Therefore, "safe" isn't exactly how most of us would assume we would feel there. Yet the Israelis live with the realization that they are in a constant state of conflict. They know that war could break out at any moment, even though everyone is talking about peace. And because of this, the Israeli government goes to great lengths when it comes to protecting visitors.

I found out after one of our flights to Israel that there were two plainclothes Israeli security men on the plane, ready to deal with anyone who would try to disrupt our safe travel. When we got to Israel the first time many years ago, two people asked us almost fifteen minutes' worth of questions about our luggage. Officials checked some of our bags. This was before an in-depth level of security had become more normative at airports.

One of the officers said to me, "I'm sorry to detain you, but over here we don't take chances. Your safety is our greatest consideration, and your enjoyment is our greatest desire."

On the streets of Israel, civilians are practically surrounded by Israeli soldiers and various security people. We were told that Israel doesn't have a high crime rate, and I can see why. The nation lives in a constant state of military readiness because its leaders understand that they are living in a potential warzone.

Even with this readiness, Israel still suffers some casualties. But imagine how much more the Israelis would suffer if they let down their guard and started living as if they didn't have an enemy in the world.

The reason there are so many casualties among believers in spiritual warfare is that we have lost sight of the fact that we are in a perpetual state of warfare, which demands constant alertness. And so we let down our guards. We open ourselves to attack. We forget that we are warriors, not tourists, in God's kingdom on earth.

An important principle to remember in life is this: just as God's kingdom is spiritual in nature, so also is Satan's. We shouldn't be surprised, therefore, that these two kingdoms clash in the spiritual realm. You don't have to be a Christian for very long to discover that the Christian life is a battleground and not a playground. This is because we are waging war in a conflict with a spiritual foe. One of Satan's strategies, though, is to get us to forget that we are fighting a spiritual battle and instead to focus on the physical, tangible challenges we face. Because so many Christians have been kept naïve of the real conflict at hand for so long, they assume people are their only problem. The Word of God teaches that what's really going on in our lives, families, churches, and the world at large is a battle that sits outside time and space, but that determines what happens in time and space. It's a spiritual battle. And although we live in a physical world, we live in a war zone. Recognizing this reality is the first step toward victory.

A KINGDOM PERSPECTIVE

We don't have all the history on the origin of this warfare, but we have enough to picture what happened and why. If we can grasp and react properly to all that the Bible teaches us about this subject, we will be alert and prepared, and we will experience a greater sense of security and peace.

But before we explore that history, let's first establish the framework of *kingdom* and how it relates to spiritual warfare. If you're like me and you grew up in America, you were regularly reminded to whom you belonged each time you said the Pledge of Allegiance or participated in the singing of our national anthem in school or before sporting and civic events. Our country didn't want us to forget that we are Americans. We recited the pledge regularly, allowing it to sink in, enabling each of us to fully understand that no matter who we were or what our background was—our history, gender, culture, or skin color—we belonged to this kingdom called the United States of America.

Even though the pledge had nothing directly to do with what was going on at that particular event or in the class-room, America wanted us to know that it was only going on, and we were only able to participate in it, because we belonged to its kingdom.

In the same way that our culture and our country wants us to be regularly reminded about our citizenship in this earthly kingdom, there is another kingdom—a greater and perfect one—of which we are a part: the kingdom of God.

Now, if you're an American citizen, it's most likely be-cause you were born here. If you're a citizen of the kingdom of God, it's because you have been born again into His king-dom. The reason you need a full comprehension of the king-dom is because it not only affects you, but also is the key to understanding the Bible. The central theme that unifies the entire Bible—from Genesis to Revelation—is the glory of God and the advancement of His kingdom.

If you don't understand that, then the Bible is simply disconnected stories that are great for inspiration but seem to be unrelated in purpose and direction. The Bible exists to reveal God's movement in history toward the establish-ment and expansion of His kingdom. Understanding that increases the relevancy of this several-thousand-year-old manuscript to your daily living because the kingdom is not only then, but now.

Throughout the Bible, the kingdom of God is His rule, His plan, His program. God's kingdom is all-encompassing. It covers everything in the universe. In fact, we can define the kingdom as God's comprehensive rule over all creation. It is the rule of God and not the rule of man that is paramount.

Now, if God's kingdom is comprehensive, so is His kingdom agenda. The kingdom agenda, then, may be defined as *the visible manifestation of the comprehensive rule of God over every area of life.*

That has serious implications for us. The reason so many of us believers are struggling is that we want God to bless our agenda rather than us to fulfill His agenda. We want God to approve our plans rather than us to accomplish His plans. We want God to bring us glory rather than us to bring Him glory.

But it doesn't work that way. God has only one plan— His kingdom agenda. We need to discover what that is so we can make sure we're working on God's plan, not ours.

The Greek word the Bible uses for "kingdom" is *basileia*, which basically means a "rule" or "authority." Included in this is the concept of power. So when we talk about a kingdom, we're talking first about a king or a ruler. We're talking about someone who's in charge. Now if there is a ruler, there also have to be "rulees" or kingdom subjects. Additionally, a kingdom includes a realm, a domain over which the king rules. Finally, if you're going to have a ruler, rulees, and a realm, you also need kingdom regulations—guidelines that govern the relationship between the ruler and the subjects.

These are necessary so that the rulees will know whether they are doing what the ruler wants.

God's kingdom includes all of these elements. He is the absolute Ruler of His domain, which encompasses all of creation. Likewise, His authority is total. Everything God rules, He runs—even when it doesn't look like He's running it. Even when life looks like it's out of control, God is running its "out-of-controlness."

God's kingdom also has its "rulees." Colossians 1:13 says that everybody who has trusted the Lord Jesus Christ as Savior has been transferred from the kingdom of darkness to the kingdom of light. If you're a believer in Jesus Christ, your allegiance has been changed. You no longer align yourself with Satan but with Christ.

To be absolutely clear, there are no in-between kingdoms and no gray areas here. There are only two realms in creation: the kingdom of God and the kingdom of Satan. We are subjects of one or the other. Everything visible and physical is always controlled or derived from that which is invisible and spiritual. Satan wants to get us to skip the divine perspective because he knows that we will never be able to solve our visible and physical problems until we address them from the divine realm. Heaven rules earth. What happens up there determines what goes on down here. So if you are not in contact with heaven, then you ought not be surprised if you are in a quandary down here on earth.

One of the greatest kings in history, Nebuchadnezzar of Babylon, learned this truth the hard way. Nebuchadnezzar had a dream that disturbed him deeply, so he asked the prophet Daniel to interpret it for him. Daniel told the king he would lose his kingdom and be driven into insanity until he learned that "it is Heaven that rules" (Dan. 4:26). What Daniel prophesied came to pass (see v. 28). God's kingdom is lived from the perspective of heaven, not earth.

Likewise, spiritual warfare is to be fought from the perspective of heaven, not earth.

GROUND ZERO

With a kingdom perspective now in place, we are ready to explore the history of our battle. To understand the origin of spiritual warfare, we have to go far back before time, into eternity past, when God created a body of beings called angels. He created them like Himself, in that they are spirit beings, for God is spirit (John 4:24).

We know that angels are magnificent beings from their appearances in Scripture. When a person saw an angel, he or she was usually overcome and fell to the ground. Angels are beings of great light, just as God's manifestations of Himself in the Bible are often accompanied by a bright light (see Acts 9). All the angels are awesome creatures, but one angel in particular was glorious.

When God created this new order of beings to worship and adore and magnify Him, He decided to create one as a special masterpiece—Lucifer, the "brilliant" or "shining one" or "star of the morning" (Isa. 14:12). Ezekiel 28 goes into more detail describing him.

We must start here because the conflict we're talking

about originated in the angelic realm before the creation described in Genesis 1. Spiritual warfare began with Lucifer's rebellion against God in heaven.

In Ezekiel 28:1–10, we're told about the king of Tyre, a human ruler who came under God's judgment because his heart was swelled with pride. He even tried to make himself like God. Then in verse 12, we're introduced to the power behind this rebellious and prideful king. It was Lucifer himself, the great being who came to be called Satan, the devil, Beelzebub, the accuser of the brethren, and so many other names and titles. Lucifer was the spiritual power influencing the king of Tyre, because, as we will see, a spiritual power always influences earthly actions because a spiritual battle is raging all around us.

Ezekiel also tells us what Lucifer was like before he rebelled against God. By understanding what he was like before his rebellion, we'll understand better why he rebelled:

> You had the seal of perfection, full of wisdom and perfect in beauty. You were in Eden, the garden of God; every precious stone was your covering: the ruby, the topaz and the diamond; the beryl, the onyx and the jasper; the lapis lazuli, the turquoise and the emerald; and the gold, the workmanship of your settings and sockets, was in you. On the day that you were created they were prepared. (Ezek. 28:12–13)

This creature shone like the brilliance of the noonday sun. He didn't have to buy diamonds to wear. He was a diamond. He was covered with every kind of precious stone. Lucifer was God's master creation. He was glorious and perfect in every detail. And he could sing! The Hebrew word "sockets" in verse 13 could be translated "pipes." Lucifer didn't just play the organ; he was the organ. When he opened his mouth to sing, he sounded like a million-dollar organ. And why not? After all, he was created to lead all the other angels in the worship and praise of God. Lucifer was blameless and flawless, a masterpiece.

Notice also that Lucifer occupied the most exalted place of all God's creatures. He was "in Eden, the garden of God." Verse 14 says, "You were on the holy mountain of God; you walked in the midst of the stones of fire." Lucifer was near God's throne; he walked in God's holy presence. His access to God was awesome, greater than that of any of the other angels. Also notice Lucifer's job title, as it were: "the anointed cherub who covers" (v. 14). The cherubs, or cherubim, are the honor guard of the angels, the angels who have the responsibility to proclaim and protect the glory of God. They are the highest rank in God's hierarchy of angels.

Lucifer was at the top of the list. He was the leader. He occupied the highest possible position that God could give to one of His creatures.

He had all of this, but then came that terrible day when, like the queen in the children's fairy tale, Lucifer stood for too long in front of a mirror. As Lucifer stood observing himself, he said, "Lucifer, you are something special! Look at that jasper. Look at these diamonds. You don't have to be number two up here. Look at all your glory. You don't have to lead the other angels in worshiping God. You deserve some of that worship yourself." Mirror, mirror on the wall was the start of the great demonic fall.

Ezekiel 28:15–17 tells us what happened next. First, Lucifer lost his perfections, his place, and his position because "unrighteousness was found in [him]" (v. 15). "Your heart was lifted up because of your beauty" (v. 17).

Lucifer's great perversion was that he took the gifts of God and made them an end in themselves. He was lifted up with the greatest of all sins: pride. He rebelled against God because he forgot something very critical—his own creatureliness.

It's mentioned a couple times in Ezekiel 28:

"On the day that you were created." (v. 13)
"From the day you were created." (v. 15)

Lucifer forgot he was a creature. He forgot that his diamonds didn't show up by themselves. He forgot that his position as the anointed cherub didn't come because he woke up one day feeling "cherubic." Lucifer forgot that the only reason he was so beautiful was that God created him that way. Lucifer stared into the mirror too long.

The angel who became Satan began to worship himself and wanted the rest of creation to worship him. That's what makes pride such a terrible sin. Pride is self-worship. It is not just feeling good about ourselves. Pride makes us feel independent of God so that we think we don't need Him. We think we are who we are because of what we have done. When this shining angel chose to act on his pride, he began a plan of rebellion, a *coup d'etat*, against the throne of God.

Lucifer went to the angels and offered them the option of following him. He did this "by the abundance of [his] trade" (Ezek. 28:16). What was his trade? His manipulating efforts among the angelic hosts.

Lucifer promoted himself, and one-third of the angels in heaven bought his platform and his plan (see Rev. 12:4). One third of the angels went with Satan and said, "Yes, you're right, we don't need God either."

Lucifer led a revolt of angels, but he failed because he found out that glory belongs to God alone. God says in Isaiah 42:8, "I am the Lord, that is My name; I will not give My glory to another." The punishment Lucifer received is recorded briefly here in Ezekiel 28. He was thrown out of heaven and cast "to the ground" (vv. 16–17). Lucifer and the demons were evicted from heaven because God will not have any challengers to His authority.

Satan's pride was the cause of his rebellion, and his judgment was its culmination. He was no longer Lucifer, the shining one.

SATAN'S PLAN

To understand the content of Satan's rebellion, the details of his plan, we need to look at Isaiah 14. We might describe the nature of the devil's rebellion as negative volition. That is, Satan made some very bad decisions in his will. We pause here to remember that God created the angels with volition, the ability to choose. He did not mandate their loyalty and obedience as if they were robots, just as He did not make us robots. Satan had a will, and according to Isaiah 14, he exercised it five times when he said, "I will."

Isaiah 14 begins with God's pronouncement of judgment against a human king, in this case the king of Babylon (vv. 4–11). Then in verse 12 we read this statement: "How you have fallen from heaven, O star of the morning, son of the dawn! You have been cut down to the earth, you who have weakened the nations!" This can be no one but the angel formerly known as Lucifer. Why did God cut Satan down to the earth? God answers that in Isaiah 14:13–14. Satan reared up in rebellion and tried to tell God how things were going to be. Let's examine Satan's five volitional statements one at a time.

"I Will Ascend to Heaven"

"But you said in your heart, 'I will ascend to heaven'" (v. 13a). Satan didn't mean he wanted to take a tour of heaven. He already had access to the highest spot in heaven, the throne of God. He was already walking among the "stones of fire" (Ezek. 28:14). He was already on the mountain of God.

So Satan was not talking about visiting heaven, but overtaking it. In other words, he wanted to ascend to heaven with a view to occupying God's throne.

"I Will Raise My Throne"

Satan's hostile intentions are obvious from his second boast: "I will raise my throne above the stars of God" (Isa. 14:13b). Job 38:7 says the stars refer to angels. Satan wanted to rule over all the angels. You may be thinking, *Wait a minute. Wasn't Satan already in charge of the angels?* Yes, he was the number one cherub, the highest-ranking angel in heaven. But Satan wasn't in charge the way God was in charge. Lucifer was saying, "Being the top angel isn't what I want. Every time I go down to the other angels, I have to tell them what God wants me to tell them. Every time I lead the angels in worship, I have to lead them to Him. Every time I meet with the other angels, the subject of our meeting is how great God is and why He deserves all the majesty and glory and worship. I'm tired of being the middleman between God and the angels. What I want is to sit on the throne, give the orders, and receive worship and glory."

Satan wanted the angels discussing him in their committee meetings. He wanted them figuring out how to serve him and make him look better. And he didn't want to answer to God anymore.

"I Will Sit on the Mount"

Satan's third boast was, "I will sit on the mount of assembly in the recesses of the north" (v. 13c). The Bible says that this mountain is the center of God's kingdom rule, where He controls the affairs of the universe (Ps. 48:2; Isa. 2:2).

Satan didn't want to pray, "Thy kingdom come, Thy will be done," but, "My kingdom come, my will be done." He wanted to be managing the kingdom.

"I Will Ascend Above the Clouds"

Then Satan said, "I will ascend above the heights of the clouds" (Isa. 14:14a). He was not talking about ascending above the clouds you see as you fly in an airplane. Many people have ascended above the clouds in airplanes. There's more to this boast than that.

The Bible associates clouds with the glory of God (Ex. 16:10; 40:34). His glory often appeared as a cloud. So clouds are those things through which the glory of God is manifested.

Satan wanted glory. He wanted praise. He tempted Jesus by showing Him the kingdoms of the world and saying, "All these things I will give You, if You fall down and worship me" (Matt. 4:9). Satan wanted to be worshiped. He still wants to be worshiped.

That's why Satan cannot hang out when we're worshiping God. He can't stand it because we're giving God that which he so desperately wants for himself. Not only that, but when we worship God, Satan is reminded of what he used to do.

Worshiping God is Satan's old job description. He used to bring God glory. But then Satan tried to share what can't be shared. He wanted to divide something that is indivisible—the glory of God. God lives for His glory, for the demonstration of His greatness. Glory means "to show off, to advertise, to put on display." God is consumed with His glory because there is no one else like Him in the universe.

The reason you and I can't get stuck on ourselves is that there is always somebody better than us, better looking than us, smarter than us, better at business than us. But God is by Himself. There is no one like Him. Nor will there ever be anyone like Him. He will share His glory with none of His creatures.

"I Will Make Myself Like the Most High"

Here is Satan's fifth and last rebellious claim: "I will make myself like the Most High" (Isa. 14:14b).

This is really the statement of a fool. Here is Satan, creature that he is, looking up at the all-knowing, all-powerful, all-present God and saying, "I'm going to be like Him."

For Satan to be like God would mean there would be two Gods. But that isn't going to happen. God says, "Before Me there was no God formed, and there will be none after Me" (Isa. 43:10). "Thus says the LORD, the King of Israel and his Redeemer, the LORD of hosts: 'I am the first and I am the last, and there is no God besides Me'" (44:6). "I am the LORD, and there is no other; besides Me there is no God" (45:5). Not a lot of room for God-making here. God cannot replicate Himself.

When Satan said he was going to become like God, he was saying he envied the independence God has. God is totally independent. He is answerable to no one outside of Himself. And God is all-knowing. Satan tempted Eve by saying that if she ate the fruit, she would have knowledge like God's (Gen. 3:5).

This idea of being like God was Satan's sin, and it was hideous. One reason it was so hideous is that he wasn't tempted to do this by anyone else. There was nobody around to tempt him. He came up with this plan all on his own.

You and I can say somebody tempted us. That doesn't exonerate us, but at least we didn't come up with the sins we commit all on our own. Yet Satan had no outside pressure. He wasn't fighting a spiritual battle against a clever enemy. He rebelled on his own.

You may wonder why God allowed Satan to rebel against Him and live to tell about it. Why didn't God crush him? We'll get into this in detail below, so let me just say here that one reason God permitted Satan's rebellion was to show the angels and us that when we don't live God's way, it doesn't work. Satan was determined to do things his way, and God let him. But the devil and his angelic and human followers will spend all eternity being reminded that rebellion against God cannot work and leads ultimately to destruction.

Yes, God permitted Satan to carry out his rebellion, but He took control of the results. Satan raised himself up against God, but God slammed him to the ground. Satan learned that although he could control his decision, he couldn't control its consequences. We need to learn that too. You may do your thing, but after you do your thing God takes over. While He gives freedom to us in our choices, God always controls the consequences.

Both Ezekiel 28 and Isaiah 14 address the consequences of judgment God carried out against His anointed cherub when Satan corrupted himself and sinned against God. When "unrighteousness was found" in Satan (Ezek. 28:15), God expelled him from "the mountain of God" and took away his place amid "the stones of fire" (v. 16). "I cast you to the ground," God told him (v. 17).

We know that the mountain of God has to do with His throne, the place from which He rules. Thus, Satan lost his privileged place near God's throne. He still has access to God's presence, as Job 1 reveals. But now he can come to God only as a "visitor." Satan has no place in heaven anymore.

The devil also lost his position as the "covering cherub" (Ezek. 28:16). The stones of fire are the angels. Satan was removed from his exalted role as head of the angels. He was also cast down to the ground, which Isaiah 14:12 tells us is the earth. Satan fell from heaven to earth, and he certainly didn't suffer his punishment happily. Revelation 12:12 warns those who dwell on the earth that Satan has come down with great anger, because he knows his time is short.

Isaiah 14:15 refers to Satan's ultimate sentence: "You will be thrust down to Sheol, to the recesses of the pit." Satan's destiny is eternal fire. Jesus stated this explicitly in Matthew 25:41. Speaking of His judgment on the Gentile nations at the end of the Tribulation, Jesus said He will pronounce this sentence to those on His left hand: "Depart from Me, accursed ones, into the eternal fire which has been prepared for the devil and his angels."

The devil's final judgment will be executed at the end of the millennial kingdom. "And the devil who deceived them was thrown into the lake of fire and brimstone, where the beast and the false prophet are also; and they will be tormented day and night forever and ever" (Rev. 20:10).

When Satan is thrown into the boiling cauldron called the lake of fire, the place of eternal torment, all those people who adopted Satan as their god will live forever with him. Hell was never made for human beings. It was created for Satan and the one-third of God's angels who rebelled with him. But many people will go there because Satan is the god they wanted.

Satan was decisively and eternally judged for his sin. The final portion of his sentence has not yet been carried out, so right now he has access to the earth and retains some of his influence. This is crucial to our understanding of spiritual warfare, because he is now our sworn enemy.

A DEMONSTRATION OF GOD'S GLORY

When God permitted Satan's sin—and then judged him and his rebellious angels—He did more than just pronounce their curse. He decided, in His eternal wisdom, to demonstrate something vitally important to these rebellious heavenly creatures.

Satan attacked God's throne and trifled with His glory, so God said to Satan, "I am going to show you something. I am going to demonstrate to you and to the angelic world My power and glory. I am going to unfold before your eyes a plan that will demonstrate I am not to be trifled with." Satan was then expelled from heaven and demoted to the earthly realm. That's the situation when we come to Genesis 1 and the beginning of creation. This is where things get interesting, because this is where spiritual warfare really began.

Notice the familiar statement in Genesis 1:2: "the earth was formless and void, and darkness was over the surface of the deep." To put it another way, earth was a wasteland. Everything was sort of floating together in a formless mass. Later, God had to separate the water from the dry land.

How did the earth become that way? It likely happened when Satan was thrown out of heaven and down to the earth (see Ezek. 28:17). Whatever Satan takes over becomes a garbage dump, including our lives.

Some Bible teachers and theologians believe that Satan's rebellion and judgment occurred between Genesis 1:1 and 1:2, so that God's perfect creation became fouled when Satan fell. I believe Satan's fall happened before Genesis 1:1, somewhere in eternity past. But here is when he was thrown down to the earth.

Either way, the earth became a place of judgment because it became the holding cell for Satan and his angels until their sentence is to be carried out.

The point is that wherever Satan resides, wherever he's in control, he creates chaos and garbage. That's why when Adam and Eve yielded to Satan, they were kicked out of Eden and the earth became a weed-filled wilderness.

Satan and his demons, the fallen angels, were limited to earth and its atmosphere as their primary realm of operation. They are still spirit beings, so they have access to the spiritual world. But their primary sphere of operation is earth.

God then decided to fix the wasteland called earth to demonstrate something very important to Satan and his demons and to the angels in heaven. Therefore, "The Spirit of God was moving over the surface of the waters" (Gen. 1:2). God began to bring order out of the chaos. He created light to counter the darkness. He separated the waters from the dry land and began to dress the earth and fill it and the sea with all kinds of creatures.

Now let me show you what happened when God began

to create. In Job 38:4–7, God asks Job where he was when God created the earth. God says when the angels saw His creative power, they "sang together" (v. 7).

Here were the angels of heaven, perhaps thousands of years after the fall of Satan had taken place. They saw light come to the dark earth, and they rejoiced. God was going to do something. What was He going to do?

God was going to make a creature of lesser stature than the angels to demonstrate to all the universe that even though this creature did not have angelic ability, angelic power, or angelic experience, if this lesser creature would trust and obey God, he would go further than an angel in heaven who refused to trust God.

Here then is the connection between Satan's rebellion and spiritual warfare. That lesser creature was mankind—you and me. God was saying to Satan, "I can take a creature of less beauty and ability than you, but who trusts Me, and I will do more with this weaker creature than you can do with all of your power."

In Psalm 8, David looked into the sky and was overwhelmed with the thought of God. He wrote:

When I consider Your heavens, the work of Your fingers,
The moon and the stars, which You have ordained;
What is man that You take thought of him,
And the son of man that You care for him?
Yet You have made him a little lower than God,
And You crown him with glory and majesty!

You make him to rule over the works of Your hands;
You have put all things under his feet. (vv. 3–6)

Verse 5 can also be translated, "Thou hast made him a little lower than the angels" (KJV), and that's the translation and interpretation I believe is called for in the context.

This is just like God. He came down to Satan's domain and said, "This earth is a wasteland. Let Me put My creative handiwork in it." God began to create, and all of a sudden, the earth was filled with light and life. Then, with Satan listening, God said, "Let Us make man in Our image" (Gen. 1:26)—just as He had made Lucifer and the angels in His image in that they were spirit beings. And God announced to Satan, "I am going to put man in charge of your house. He will have dominion over the earth, and rule over the birds of the air and the fish of the sea."

That explains why the serpent came to Eve and tempted her to doubt God. Satan wanted the planet. Adam and Eve gave it to him by their sin. And guess what God is in the process of doing today through His people? He is taking this planet back from Satan. This is His plan: to display His power and glory to the angels of heaven and to Satan and the demons of hell.

Here's another key to God's plan. Satan and the angels who followed him spurned God's goodness and grace. So God wanted to show them the glory of His grace when it is received by repentant sinners. God permitted sin in order that His grace might be shown to be greater (see Rom. 5:20). But this display of grace did something more. It allowed God to express His love while satisfying His demand for justice at the same time.

God can't just skip sin. Yet God loves us. How can He satisfy His justice that must deal with sin and also satisfy His love? God did so by putting our sins on Jesus and punishing Him, thereby satisfying His holiness that demands that sin be paid for. Christ's death freed God to show His loving and forgiving grace to sinners who come to Him, confess their sins, and receive Jesus as Savior. This is the manifold wisdom of God.

God also permitted sin to demonstrate that there is no meaning or hope in life apart from Him. He permitted Satan and us to have the ability to choose so that He could secure our obedience and service out of love, not out of fear. God doesn't want people to love and serve Him because they're afraid He is going to smite them if they don't. What God did in creation was to parallel man's situation with that of Satan. Satan was created a perfect being with a free will and the ability to choose. Adam was created a perfect being with a free will and the ability to choose.

Lucifer's heavenly homestead was called Eden (see Ezek. 28:13). Adam's earthly homestead was also called Eden. Lucifer was to oversee all of God's angelic creation; Adam was to oversee all of God's earthly creation. Lucifer had direct access to God in heaven; Adam had direct access to God when they walked together in the garden.

Mankind would parallel Satan and his angels in another way. The Bible says there are two classes of angels: elect angels and fallen angels. There will be two classifications of mankind: saved and unsaved, elect and fallen.

God created mankind to rule the earth. Satan came to Adam and Eve to take over earth. That's one major reason why God had to become a man in the person of Jesus Christ, because a man had to take the earth back from Satan. What we're experiencing on earth in terms of spiritual warfare has to do with something that is much bigger than we are.

Friend, if you want to correct the effects of Satan's rebellion in your life, you must learn that God will go to enormous lengths to guard and preserve His glory. God will spare nothing to preserve His glory. If you try to interfere with God's glory, if you try to take from God that which belongs to Him alone, you are in trouble. A lot of people in the Bible had to learn that the hard way.

Remember King Nebuchadnezzar of Babylon (Dan. 4:28–37). If he were here, he might tell you, "Don't ever do what I did, standing on my balcony talking about 'Look at this great Babylon that I have built.' Don't ever do that, because my nails started to grow, and hair started growing out all over me. I crawled like an animal for seven years, but I learned my lesson. When I got my sanity back, I let it be known that there's only one God. He will bring you down to the dirt on your face, if He has to, to teach you this lesson."

This is why the serpent who tempted Eve was sentenced to crawl on his belly (Gen. 3:14). The serpent was used by Satan to steal the glory of God in the lives of Adam and Eve. And when you steal the glory of God, God will put you on your face, so to speak. You'll be crawling in the dust until you give Him back His glory.

Ask King Herod Agrippa I (Acts 12:20–23). Herod took the podium to speak, and the people said, "The voice of a god and not of a man!" (v. 22). Herod liked that. He said, "Yes, I am a god." But he was immediately eaten by worms and died because he did not give God the glory. There is no room in the universe for two Gods.

The Bible tells us to humble ourselves before God (James 4:10; 1 Peter 5:6). Pride is one of the preeminent weapons of the enemy. Be on guard against it. It brought Satan down. It has the power to bring you down too.

This is spiritual warfare. This is our battle. You were born a warrior, whether or not you want to be one. If you want to position yourself for victory, you must rightly understand the history, nature, and strategy of the enemy.

2

The Expansion
of the Battle

God set His plan in motion when He created Adam and Eve and told them to rule over the earth. Until this point, the battle had been confined to the heavenly realm and the participants were all spirit beings. But when God made Adam and Eve, the battle expanded to the earth and the list of combatants expanded to include the human race. This all happened in Genesis 3, in which we find Satan's plan to take over the earth.

But before we consider Genesis 3, which is crucial to understanding spiritual warfare, we need to back up just a bit and set the stage for Satan's attack against our first parents. You'll remember that one facet of Lucifer's creation was his volition, or freedom of choice. God created all the angels with the ability to choose because He wants His creatures to serve Him out of love, not out of requirement. Lucifer made his choice and became the devil.

God also created man and woman with the power of choice for the same reason. Adam and Eve had the ability to choose whether they would love and obey God or disobey Him. To make their choice real and not just potential, God planted some trees in Eden. According to Genesis 2:9, God filled Eden with every kind of tree imaginable for Adam's enjoyment and for food. And in the middle of the garden, God planted two particular trees: the Tree of Life and the Tree of Knowledge of Good and Evil. In Genesis 2:16–17, we read God's instructions regarding the forbidden tree, the Tree of Knowledge of Good and Evil. If Adam ate from it, he would "surely die." The Hebrew text is emphatic about this.

What God was doing was re-creating the conditions of the original spiritual battle in heaven. That is, He placed His perfect creatures, Adam and Eve, in a perfect environment, with everything they could ever want. We know they were perfect because Genesis 2:25 says they were completely unashamed at their nakedness. They had no reason to be ashamed.

The point is that God now had a creature through whom He would demonstrate His power and His saving grace. But in order for God's grace to be made manifest, mankind had to have the power of choice. And in order for God to demonstrate His infinitely superior power, mankind had to be included in this angelic conflict called spiritual warfare.

This brings us to Genesis 3. Here was God's innocent couple, newly married, ready to serve Him. Satan had to make his move. Why? If Adam and Eve made the right choice, they would live forever, the battle would be over, the victory would be won, and time—and Satan—would be no more.

Satan did not want that to happen, so he came after Eve. But why did he wait until Eve was created to launch his attack? Because he wasn't just after Adam. Satan wanted to destroy the entire race by destroying the progenitors of the race. He understood something we have forgotten, which is that whoever owns the family owns the future.

Satan wasted no time in expanding the war. As soon as God's instructions concerning the tree were given and Adam and Eve were married, Satan moved in to try to spoil God's plan and take back what he thought was his.

Let's look at Genesis 3:1–7 to learn about Satan's mode of attack, because it's the same basic strategy he uses against us today.

QUESTIONING GOD'S AUTHORITY

"Now the serpent was more crafty than any beast of the field which the Lord God had made" (v. 1a). Satan knows how to dress for war. Forget the picture of a guy with horns and a long tail, wearing a red jumpsuit and carrying a pitchfork. Satan used a serpent, which apparently was an attractive creature at this point, to approach Eve.

Notice that the first conversation between a human being and the devil was about God. Why? Because this is a *spiritual* battle, and mankind was thrust right into the middle of it. You and I are still there, by the way.

Satan began his efforts by questioning God's authority.

The primary component upon which all else rests in a kingdom is the authority of the ruler. Without that, there is anarchy, which ultimately leads to utter chaos. This is exactly why Satan's very first move in the garden was to subtly and deceitfully dethrone the Ruler.

Before we read about Satan approaching Eve in the garden, every reference to God in Scripture in relation to Adam is made as "Lord God." Anytime you read the word Lord (in all caps), it refers to the name used for God which is *Yahweh. Yahweh* literally means "master, and absolute ruler" and is the name God used to reveal Himself to mankind regarding His relationship with him. Yet before Adam was made, God revealed Himself in Scripture as Creator, which is the name Elohim.

However, when Satan spoke to Eve about eating that which she could not have, he did not refer to God as "Lord God." Essentially, he stripped off the name Lord—removing "master, and absolute ruler"—and instead said, "Indeed, has God said . . . ?" (Gen. 3:1). Thus Satan sought to reduce God's rulership over mankind by beginning with the subtle yet incredibly impactful twist to His name. In doing so, Satan kept the concept of religion while eliminating divine authority. By removing "Lord" from the authoritative nature of the relationship between God and humanity, and in bypassing Adam by going directly to Eve, Satan not only caused mankind to rebel, but also took over the dominion that man was supposed to be exercising underneath God's authority. When both Adam and Eve ate from the fruit in disobedience, they chose to change how they viewed their Creator from *Lord God* to simply *God*. As a result, they lost not only their intimate fellowship with Him and each other, but also their power of the dominion that flows from the ultimate Ruler of the domain.

And even though Eve ate the fruit first, God went looking for Adam. It had been Adam to whom God had revealed Himself as "Lord God," in the context of giving Adam his divine instruction. As a result, when the title of "master, and absolute ruler" got removed, it was Adam who was ultimately held responsible.

Ever since, a battle has continuously raged over who will rule mankind. This is because Adam's importance wasn't simply that he was the first man God made. Rather, Adam was to be the prototype of which all men were to become. Therefore, when men and women make decisions based on their own thoughts, beliefs or values—like Adam did—rather than based on what God has to say as Ruler, they are choosing to rule themselves. They are choosing to call the King "God" without recognizing His authority by removing His rightful name "Lord God" or "Lord God" (lowercase "Lord") also found in Scripture, referring to *Adown* ("master")—the verbal parallel to *Yahweh*. Like Adam, they essentially are seeking to dethrone their Creator while still recognizing His existence. It is religion without the ruler relationship of *Yahweh*.

There are two answers to every question: God's answer and everyone else's. Removing the title of "master" and "absolute ruler" from a person's relationship to God essentially places God's answer on the same level as everyone else's. Adam's sin was in allowing human viewpoint, which had been initiated by Satan, to override the revealed will and Word of God—even though the viewpoint came from his wife. Adam allowed a person close to him to overrule God. Satan had come at Adam and Eve with a subtle attack that cast doubt on God's rightful authority. He was so successful with this in the Garden of Eden that he has been using the same strategy ever since. Only by putting "LORD" back into the equation—recognizing Him as the ultimate ruler who gives you the dominion and authority you were created to have—will you gain victory in spiritual warfare.

QUESTIONING GOD'S WORD

Satan's next approach to Eve, after denying God's rightful authority, was to turn God's clear statement into a question: "Indeed, has God said, 'You shall not eat from any tree of the garden'?" (v. 1b). Satan was basically saying, "Eve, has God placed any limitations on you? Has He said no to you about anything in the garden? Is God being cruel and unfair to you? Are you suffering unnecessarily because God is being hard on you?"

Do you see the cleverness of the devil's strategy? God had said that Adam and Eve could eat freely from all the trees of the garden, except one. But Satan did not bring up the vastness of God's goodness. The devil wanted to discuss only the one restriction God had placed on mankind. Satan always does this. He focuses on the one time God says no rather than on the many times God says yes. People think of the Ten Commandments as mostly negative. But the fact is that every time God says, "You shall not," He is saying, "You shall" to a whole list of legitimate things. For instance, when God says, "You shall not covet," He is saying, "You are free to fully enjoy the things you acquire legitimately." But Satan camps on the prohibition and causes us to ignore all the good gifts God gives us.

Most parents have experienced this phenomenon at one time or another with their children—and often at Christmas. Say your children give you a wish list of ten toys, and you buy nine of them. On Christmas morning, they open the nine gifts you bought them because you love them. But instead of saying, "Thank you for these nine great toys," the only thing they can say is, "Where is number ten?"

Questioning God's Word is the devil's trick to get you to overlook and underappreciate God's goodness. That's why Paul says that when you come to God in prayer about a need in your life, you are to come *with thanksgiving* to make your request known to God (Phil. 4:6). Even when you're worried or despondent, you are to come to God saying, "Thank You, Father, for who You are, for all that You have done for me, for Your grace that has saved me, for the answers to prayer I have seen in my life." That's what it looks like to come to Him "with thanksgiving."

But what do we do more often? We come to God with the attitude, "Why haven't You done this for me yet?" God's response is, "When you come to Me, start with all the good things I have done for you. Start with all the trees I have provided for you to eat from." God wants us to come to Him with praise and thanksgiving because He has put a lot of trees out there for us to enjoy. But Satan always wants to get us hung up on the one tree we can't have.

So Satan asked Eve, "Has God put any limitations on you?"

Eve responded, "From the fruit of the trees of the garden we may eat; but from the fruit of the tree which is in the middle of the garden, God has said, 'You shall not eat from it or touch it, or you will die'" (Gen. 3:2–3).

We know Eve is in trouble already, because she's talking with the devil over what God said. And in doing so, she changes God's words at least three times.

First, Eve failed to mention that God said she and Adam could "freely" eat from all the other trees in the garden (2:16). That word "freely" is very important because God was saying, "All of creation is available to you at no cost. You may eat freely, abundantly, to your heart's content. I have provided all this for you." God wasn't just good to Adam and Eve; He was *very* good. It didn't cost them anything. In making that omission, Eve minimized God's good provision.

Second, Eve added the prohibition against touching the fruit. God never said anything about not touching it. Why is this important? Because Eve was essentially turning God into a legalist, into a cruel killjoy who wouldn't even let her get near enough to the forbidden tree to feel its bark, let alone eat its fruit. So many people think the Christian life is simply, "You can't do this and you can't do that." That makes God look stale and miserly, not someone you'd want to follow gladly into spiritual battle.

Eve's third change to God's Word is a slight variation on

the judgment He announced. God did not say, "Don't eat or you will die," as Eve said to the devil. That makes the judgment sound like merely a possibility: maybe you will die, maybe you won't. Eve thus weakened the penalty. But God's word of judgment in Genesis 2:17 was much stronger than what she portrayed. "You shall surely die." This is emphatic. Adam and Eve were certain to die if they disobeyed. God's judgment was guaranteed.

Satan had driven a wedge of doubt into Eve's heart and mind. He had her wondering why God was withholding that one tree from her. She was about to forget the goodness and provision of God and start focusing on His one restriction.

Now Satan was ready to deliver his major strike. He flatly contradicted what God said. "The serpent said to the woman, 'You surely will not die!'" (3:4). Here, Satan challenged God's truthfulness. "What God said won't really happen. He wasn't telling you the truth."

Satan didn't stop after delivering his frontal attack. He went on to tell Eve his version of what the real problem was. "God knows that in the day you eat from it your eyes will be opened, and you will be like God, knowing good and evil" (v. 5). In other words, the devil was saying, "Let me tell you what God is really doing here. God knows something He doesn't want you to know. You can be like Him." What did Satan want more than anything else? To be like God. He was trying to get Eve to repeat his sin. This was a powerful temptation. "God is holding out on you, Eve. He's being selfish. He wants to be God all by Himself. But let me tell you the secret, girl. The answer is in this tree. If you take a bite of its fruit, you will know what God knows. You will be as powerful as He is. God doesn't want that to happen. But how would you like to be equal with God?"

Satan knew exactly what he was doing. The Tree of Knowledge of Good and Evil, standing in the middle of the garden, was a daily reminder to Adam and Eve that they were creatures, not the Creator. They had to obey and answer to a higher authority. That's the same thing that bothered Satan. He had an exalted position. God had created him more beautiful than any other creature. But he was still a creature and not God.

So now the devil was trying to make Eve chafe under her restriction the way he chafed under his. By offering Eve the forbidden fruit, Satan invited mankind to join him in his rebellion. The spiritual warfare Satan launched in heaven was about to be expanded to earth.

As Eve listened to the serpent's line, she looked at the Tree of Knowledge of Good and Evil. "When the woman saw that the tree was good for food, and that it was a delight to the eyes, and that the tree was desirable to make one wise, she took from its fruit and ate; and she gave also to her husband with her, and he ate" (Gen. 3:6). This wasn't the first time Eve had seen this tree, but it was the first time she had seen it through Satan's eyes. That was the difference. That's what Satan always does with sin. He wants to get us to see sin through his eyes. He wants to deceive us. As we will see later, this is his primary weapon.

The longer Eve looked at that tree, the more she just had to taste its fruit. She wanted to be what Satan wanted to be.

She wanted to be like God. So she took the fruit and ate it. And then she said, "Adam, come here. I'm not going down by myself. This is a family thing." And he ate, too.

The minute Adam and Eve ate the forbidden fruit, they died just as God had promised. They became spiritually dead and alienated from God, just as Satan was alienated from God. They fell under the curse of sin. And our first parents knew right away that something was wrong. "The eyes of both of them were opened, and they knew that they were naked; and they sewed fig leaves together and made themselves loin coverings" (v. 7).

Sin produced immediate results. The Bible says that when Adam and Eve disobeyed, their fellowship with each other was broken. They were now conscious and ashamed of their nakedness. They hid their bodies from each other. More important, their fellowship with God was broken because the next time God came looking for them, Adam and Eve "hid themselves from the presence of the LORD God among the trees of the garden" (v. 8). They were now living in fear and shame. Their innocence was lost.

They had good reason to hide because Adam's conversation with God in 3:9–12 brought out the truth: "I ate." The first humans disobeyed God because they let their feelings and desires take precedence over God's revelation. Eve felt like she just had to have a piece of that fruit. Adam followed his feelings, too. There's nothing wrong with your feelings, but your feelings should never cause you to lose sight of God's Word. Our feelings must be aligned with His revelation.

Adam and Eve coveted something that was not theirs: the knowledge and glory of God. Satan is still tempting people to covet things that don't belong to them. We need to pay close attention here because Genesis 3 teaches us a lot about the spiritual warfare we face every day.

In one blink of time, the human race was handed over to the evil one. Satan and mankind were now united against God in spiritual battle. So God began to take the situation in hand. He went down the line, pronouncing a curse against each participant in this first battle on earth.

The serpent was the first to be cursed. "On your belly you will go, and dust you will eat" (3:14). God told this creature, "Do you want to be with the devil? Fine. I'm going to put you down on your face in the dust where Satan is." Verse 15 is part of the serpent's curse, but I want to save it for later because it's a special verse.

Eve's curse was a painful one: "I will greatly multiply your pain in childbirth, in pain you will bring forth children; yet your desire will be for your husband, and he will rule over you" (v. 16). The last phrase of that verse is controversial, but the curse fits the sin. Eve took over, grabbing the reins of leadership from her husband. She acted independently of Adam. So God's judgment of Eve was twofold. First, she would experience pain in childbirth. Every labor pain would become a reminder of her rebellion. Every birth pang would remind Eve of what she forgot, which was the same thing Satan forgot—that she was the creature, not the Creator. She was not God.

Second, her desire would be for her husband. Many

commentators take the word *desire* to mean that a woman would have a natural sexual desire for her husband even though the result, childbirth, was painful. But I don't believe God was talking about that desire. Eve had desired to dominate Adam, so her curse was to be dominated or ruled over by Adam. To put it in blunt terms, man would dominate woman. Man would subjugate woman, be insensitive to woman. Does that excuse men who abuse women? Of course not! That's sin, and abusers are responsible before God for it. But every time you see an insensitive and domineering husband, it's a reminder of what happens when we mess with the Creator's plan. Spiritual warfare has not only a vertical dimension, between God and Satan. It has a horizontal dimension, between people.

Adam was the last to hear his curse: "Cursed is the ground because of you; in toil you will eat of it all the days of your life. . . . By the sweat of your face you will eat bread, till you return to the ground" (3:17, 19).

Adam and Eve acted independently of God by eating the fruit. So, God said to Adam, "Since you want to eat independently of Me, I am going to make it hard for you to eat now. You will have to work hard and sweat to earn your food."

When Adam and Eve let God feed them, He fed them abundantly and freely. But there were no more free meals now. Adam would have to go out and wrestle his food out of a cursed ground. He was going to have to work for a living. Every time a man comes home tired from a hard day's labor, he needs to remember Adam. Although work itself was instituted before the fall, hard work is a perpetual reminder that when you rebel against God, there's no more Paradise, no more eating freely from God's abundant garden full of trees.

This scene of judgment teaches us an important lesson for spiritual warfare: Rebelling against God isn't fun. All of a sudden, the thrill is gone. All of a sudden, that tree wasn't nearly as alluring to Eve as it had looked before. Now that chaos and destruction had set in, sin looked as ugly as it really is. Not only that, but when Adam and Eve were obedient to God, God picked up the tab for their needs. But when they acted independently of God and imitated Satan's rebellion, they had to pay their own tab. And the price was very, very heavy.

Thus God turned the earth over to mankind. But then Satan overturned that by tempting mankind to sin and by bringing the human race and the earth under his dominion. God could have wiped out the whole mess in judgment, but He had a better plan.

Now we're ready for the best part of the story.

God told the serpent, through whom Satan was working, "I will put enmity between you and the woman, and between your seed and her seed; he shall bruise you on the head, and you shall bruise him on the heel" (3:15). A man from the seed of woman—Jesus Christ—would one day crush and destroy Satan. In other words, God said, "Satan, this battle is not over. It may appear that you won this round. But I am not going to change My plan. I am still going to work through a human seed." So, the situation now is that the world contains two distinct seeds, two offspring: the children of the devil who follow him, and the children of

God who obey Him. These two lines are so diametrically opposed that they cannot help but be at enmity with each other, just as God and Satan are at enmity with each other. This means that our warfare on earth is a reflection of warfare in heaven. God guaranteed that His seed would win the final victory, but Satan—being the tireless adversary that he is—said, in effect, "We'll see about that, God. This war is not over. It will be my seed against Your seed from now on. I'm going to get started on my seed right away."

And he did. Genesis 6:1–4 describes a unique event. Scholars have not reached a consensus regarding what exactly is going on in this passage or the precise identity of the figures mentioned in it, but this is what I believe: Satan sent "the sons of God," a group of his fallen angels, to inhabit ungodly men, who would cohabit with human women and produce a race of men called "Nephilim." Then the text says, "the wickedness of man was great on the earth" (v. 5). The sons of God were the angels of Jude 6, those who did not keep to their own domain. They got together with women and had children who were evil and demonic. Satan was attempting to produce his own seed, his offspring. God judged these wicked angels by confining them in the abyss, but Satan has been trying to develop his seed ever since.

Adam had been judged, but God had another word for him (Gen. 3:20–21). Adam heard God's prophecy of a coming Savior (v. 15), and then the text says he named his wife Eve, "because she was the mother of all *the* living" (v. 20). The last "the" in this verse is italicized, meaning it wasn't in the original language. Adam called his wife Eve because she was "the mother of all living." That's a powerful verse. I believe Adam was saying, "God, I trust that You are going to produce through my wife a seed that will crush the devil's head. And the way You know I believe You is by the name I'm giving to my wife. She will be called Eve, the mother of all people, including the living One who will someday win the battle with the devil and crush him."

Then in verse 21, we read, "The LORD God made garments of skin for Adam and his wife, and clothed them." God provided a sacrifice to cover their nakedness—and to cover their sin. Follow the sequence here: God judged Adam because he sinned. Adam would have to work the ground by his sweat until he died and returned to the dust himself. But God also said there was going to be a seed of the woman who would engage Satan in spiritual warfare and, unlike Adam, emerge victorious. Adam heard this and said, "God, I believe You. I'm going to name my wife in light of my belief that she will produce the seed who will fulfill Your promise." So God said, "Because you have exercised faith, I am going to replace the leaves you sewed together by your own effort with My covering. Your covering will never work. Your covering will not solve the problem of sin. But I have a covering that will fix the problem."

Then God killed an animal, shedding its blood as a substitute for Adam and Eve, and took the animal's skin and wrapped it around the two in the garden. Now they had divinely provided covering rather than humanly provided covering. God covered them in His righteousness, rather than letting them stay covered in their own righteousness—which really was no righteousness at all.

People have been trying to come up with their own covering for sin since the garden. But the only thing that can cover you before a holy God is His covering. That's why all the way through the Old Testament, the people offered animal sacrifices. They were covering their sin before a holy God until the seed of the woman, Jesus Christ (see Gal. 3:16; 4:4), would come and provide a permanent sacrifice through His own blood.

This contest is the real heart of spiritual warfare—and the good news is that it's no contest! Because Jesus Christ is God, He could not help but emerge victorious. And to show us how we can win over Satan just as Jesus won over Satan, God allowed His Son to be tempted by the devil (Matt. 4:1–11). Jesus beat the devil in the desert by using the Word of God. Remember that in Genesis 3, Satan attacked the Word of God and defeated Adam and Eve. But in the desert, Jesus—the "last Adam" (1 Cor. 15:45)—used the Word to win over Satan. Jesus did everything right where the first Adam did everything wrong. Adam ate outside of God's will. Jesus refused to do so. Adam disobeyed God's Word. Jesus obeyed it perfectly. What the first Adam messed up, the last Adam fixed. Nobody but Jesus could have been the seed of the woman. All men were fallen in sin.

At just the right time, Jesus was born of a virgin and came into this world to be our Savior, our Deliverer, and our victory over Satan, sin, and hell. The spiritual battle is already over and won! But Satan continues to fight, and he wants to take as many people down with him as he can. We must stand against him and defeat him the same way Jesus defeated him—through the power and Word of God—and by aligning our hearts, minds, and actions underneath the comprehensive rule of God over every area of life. We must submit to His kingdom agenda.

This is our battle. In this is our victory.

3

The Battlefront

I t's easy to be a soldier in a television show or film. The weapons aren't loaded, there is no enemy to be found, and all your leader has to do is make sure you keep in step. But when you're in a war, your weapons are always loaded, the enemy is in sight (or soon to be), and your commander is telling you what to do in order to stay alive and win the battle.

Too many believers in Jesus Christ act as if they are a soldier onscreen instead of in a real war. They dress up nice, smile and wave, and want to know how to keep in step rather than how to go to war. That's why we have so many casualties on the spiritual battlefield. You can't fight a war while marching in nice, straight lines. The British redcoats learned that when they came to the American colonies.

Someone might say, "How do you know we're in a war?" That's easy. Besides the casualties, we also have a lot of prisoners of war, believers who have been taken captive by the enemy in some area of their lives.

As we've seen, God created mankind to rule the earth and demonstrate His power to Satan and the angelic world. But due to the fall, "the whole world lies in the power of the evil one" (1 John 5:19). Satan has an agenda: to keep the world of unsaved people under his control and render Christians ineffective in spiritual warfare, bringing us down to daily defeat. He seeks to carry out his agenda through four specific fronts of attack. Since the Garden of Eden, he has widened the battle to include all of life, and he is attacking on all four fronts simultaneously.

THE INDIVIDUAL FRONT

The devil's first battlefront is our individual lives. The apostle Peter said, "Be of sober spirit, be on the alert. Your adversary, the devil, prowls around like a roaring lion, seeking someone to devour" (1 Peter 5:8). To put it bluntly, Satan is after *you*. No matter who you are or what your status is, he wants to overthrow and defeat you. I referred above to Christian prisoners of war. The devil has some Christians in POW camps due to alcohol, drugs, pornography, fear, discouragement, depression, pride, narcissism, materialism, and a whole host of other problems. There are lots of names for these things. But in the spiritual realm, the fact is that believers who are being held captive by the devil in things like these are prisoners of war. The devil is after individual Christians, seeking to capture and destroy them spiritually.

THE FAMILY FRONT

The second front where Satan attacks God's people is in their family life. We saw this in the garden when Satan tempted Eve. Eve gave the fruit to Adam, and the family came under the authority of hell. We saw it in Genesis 6, when a group of fallen angels cohabited with women and produced offspring as part of Satan's plan to create a demonic family and race.

It should be obvious why the family is so important to Satan. According to God's curse on the serpent in Genesis 3, from then on, the battle would be waged between the seed of the woman and the seed of the serpent. The offspring of these two lines, the godly line and the ungodly line, is key to the fight.

That means Satan wants to destroy your family. He wants to destroy you and the next generation too. If Satan can get to the next generation by messing up our homes, then he has us, our kids, and the homes they will establish someday, because our children will be ill equipped to raise their children properly. Spiritual warfare, then, becomes a generational problem.

This is why Satan loves to see divorce among Christian couples. If he can get husbands and wives fighting each other over their disagreements and personality conflicts and preferences, then they will miss the bigger battle altogether. Their conflict is not just about their personalities and so forth; it's about war in the spiritual realm. The tragedy is that many of us Christians are still fighting flesh and blood rather than the principalities and powers and world forces that are devastating us (Eph. 6:12). We must fight for the family because whoever controls the family controls the future. That's why Satan wants your family and mine.

THE CHURCH FRONT

The enemy also attacks on a third front, the church. Here he promotes disunity, division, and discrimination through things such as personality squabbles and power struggles, and through more serious problems such as doctrinal error, racism, chauvinism, and culturalism. Satan wants to divide the family of God because he understands something that many Christians don't: often, God doesn't work in a context of disunity. If the body of Christ is going to see the power of God fully in action, then we must be of one heart and one mind. If our enemy can split God's people along racial, class, gender, or cultural lines, if he can get people making decisions based on personal bias rather than on divine truth, he has won a major battle.

But when you're in a war, you don't care about the color, class, gender, or culture of the person fighting next to you, as long as he or she is shooting in the same direction you are. We're in a common battle against a common enemy, so we'd better learn to get along and fight together.

One reason our communities are in disarray is that the churches in these communities have not come together to bring the power of God to bear on their problems. And one reason that churches have not come together is that we're not good at distinguishing between membership and discipleship. Membership involves a simple formal inclusion into the existing entity and often carries with it little to no responsibility. Discipleship, on the other hand, involves the transformation of individuals into the likeness and character of Jesus Christ. When that occurs, love—the foundational commandment Christ gave (Matt. 22:37–38)—will be reflected in all we do and say. Paul said we must be "diligent to preserve the unity of the Spirit in the bond of peace" (Eph. 4:3). Satan wants to attack and disjoin the church, because if he can do that, he negates divine power.

THE SOCIETY FRONT

In Daniel 10:13–14, we get a glimpse of Satan's activity on a fourth front, the society at large. In this passage, an angel reveals to the prophet Daniel that Satan is the energizing force behind the rulers of the nations. To be clear, I'm not saying that all human rulers are demonically inspired. It's easy to see Satan's power behind a Hitler or a Stalin, and behind the various dictators and warlords who are destroying lives and nations today. Thankfully, not every nation is ruled by people like that. But it's important to recognize a spiritual warfare principle here. Since it's true that the whole world lies in Satan's power, then we have to recognize he exerts influence over the world's leaders and structures.

Once we understand this principle, we realize that the answer to our culture's woes lies much deeper than just electing the right person to office. That's certainly important, but there is a bigger battle going on here. Until we begin to trace our individual, familial, church, and societal problems back to their spiritual source, Satan will continue to take spiritual POWs—and in bunches. You may feel that Satan has taken you prisoner in one or more of these areas. Your problem may go all the way back to childhood in the form of an abusive parent. You may be repeating destructive patterns in your family that were present in your birth home.

Whatever the case, you may have been a prisoner of war for so long that you think and act like a POW. Identifying Satan's areas of attack is one important step toward being liberated. Another is to find out how he attacks us.

SATAN'S METHOD OF ATTACK

Satan knows not only *where* to get at us, but also *how* to get at us. We'll explore this in more detail in the next chapter, but it is helpful to discuss it briefly here. We need to understand the method he uses to defeat and imprison us.

In 2 Corinthians 10:3–5, Paul reveals the devil's primary battle strategy:

> Though we walk in the flesh, we do not war according to the flesh, for the weapons of our warfare are not of the flesh, but divinely powerful for the destruction of fortresses. We are destroying speculations and every lofty thing raised up against the knowledge of God, and we are taking every thought captive to the obedience of Christ.

What Paul wants us to know first is that we can't use secular or fleshly weapons to fight spiritual battles. The reason so many Christians are losing the battle is that they are trying to beat the devil using the world's weapons. They're looking to the secular world to help them with their spiritual need. If your problem, your struggle, your need is induced and orchestrated by your spiritual enemy, your flesh can't win the fight. Unless you choose a spiritual response, all the time, effort, and resources you spend trying to fix the problem will ultimately be a waste of time, a Band-Aid on the situation.

Paul says our methods are not of the flesh because our enemy is not of the flesh. Some of us have been wrestling with things day in and day out for years. Those are battles, no matter what other name we may give to them. And if God speaks to it, it is a spiritual battle. And if your battle is spiritual, it needs a spiritual cure. You don't fight cancer with skin lotion. You don't fight a brain tumor by taking aspirin and lying down. Those kinds of problems demand other kinds of help. So do spiritual problems.

The text we cited above tells us that Satan targets his attacks on our minds, because Paul talks about "speculations," "the knowledge of God," and "taking every thought captive" (2 Cor. 10:5). Where do speculations come from? The mind. Where is knowledge rooted? In the mind. Where do thoughts come from? The mind. It is all in the mind. So, the Christian who wants to trade his or her spiritual POW status for freedom must learn to think differently.

When Satan attacks a Christian's mind, he starts building what Paul calls "fortresses" ("strongholds," NIV and KJV).

The devil builds a place from which he can operate, and he means for that fortress to be permanent. He plans to take up residency there.

Satan makes himself at home, in other words, and he gets a grip on the mind until people begin thinking there is no way to overcome this problem, no way to save this marriage, no way to unify this church, no way to make a difference in our world. Whenever you hear a Christian saying, "No way. It can't be done. I've tried everything, and it just doesn't work," you're looking at somebody who has allowed Satan to build a fortress in the mind. However that fortress got there, it was constructed by the evil one.

A fortress or stronghold is a mindset that holds you hostage. It makes you believe that you are hopelessly locked in a situation, that you are powerless to change. That's when you hear people saying, "I can't, I can't, I can't." The only reason you say, "I can't," when God says, "You can," is that Satan has made himself at home in your head. In computer terms, he has you operating by the old information that was on the hard drive of your mind before you became a Christian. The Bible teaches that before we were saved, we were operating by a godless way of thinking, a vain and empty thought system. Satan controlled the keyboard that entered data into our minds and put it on the screen of our lives to be lived out.

But when we came to faith in Jesus Christ, He gave us a new drive in our minds with new data to control the way we live. Every believer has this new data, but many of us are still living by the old data that will not be erased completely until we get to heaven. Even though we are on our way to heaven, we are still being programmed by the enemy in some areas. That's why Paul had to write this passage in 2 Corinthians. He wanted to help believers who had become trapped into thinking the enemy's way—which all of us have done at one time or another.

How is Satan able to pull off this kind of influence in a Christian's mind? He does it by raising up "lofty thing[s]" (2 Cor. 10:5). A lofty thing is a partition, a wall. We have a couple of classrooms in our church building that have partitions we can pull to divide a large classroom into two rooms. The reason for drawing a partition is to keep the two activities or classes on each side from mixing with each other. Why does Satan want to raise up a partition in our minds? Because he wants us to be what James 1:8 calls "double-minded" people. The idea is to divide our minds. When this happens, we keep that which is of God on one side and that which is not of God on the other. We literally have two minds—two sides of the room, if you will.

Satan's partitions are "raised up against the knowledge of God" (2 Cor. 10:5). Satan wants to block divine information from crossing over to the other side of your brain. He wants to block the knowledge of God in your life, to keep it from infiltrating the other side of the room.

That way, you can go to church with your problem or your sin and hear the Word of God. But when Satan raises the partition, the biblical data you heard on Sunday are not transferred to Monday. So you come to church with your problem and leave with your problem, and all you had in between was a nice song and a sermon. Satan erected his partition and blocked the knowledge of God.

Satan wants to block the knowledge of God in your life for the same reason he wanted to block the knowledge of God in Eve's life. He knows that if you ever take God seriously, you're going to live life as God meant it to be lived. And the devil doesn't want that. Instead, he wants to keep your mind divided. He wants to make you a spiritual schizophrenic, someone who can smile and praise God in church and then be a completely different person out in the parking lot. A schizophrenic saint stands up for Jesus in church yet is a "secret saint" at work. Nobody knows that this person belongs to Christ. He is for God one minute and for himself the next.

Satan wants you to have two minds. A person with two minds is never really sure who the enemy is. He is a confused and ineffective spiritual warrior. We cannot let Satan build strongholds in our minds and divide our thinking. God's thoughts must always be superimposed over our thoughts.

Satan's attack plan is to get to our minds and erect barriers that keep us from obeying God and enjoying victory. But Paul tells us that we can counterattack and destroy Satan's attempts to build a base of operations in our lives.

Satan wants to build his fortress in your mind, but he needs a piece of ground to build it on. But you don't have to yield any ground to him. God has given you and me the power to counter Satan's attack, to overrun and destroy his fortresses.

Back in 2 Corinthians 10:4, Paul says our spiritual weapons—which we will discuss at length in chapter 9—can destroy Satan's fortresses. Weapons such as prayer, reading the Word, obedience, meditation on Scripture, fasting, and service can blow up the devil's strongholds. And that's what we must do. These fortresses don't need to be remodeled. God doesn't tell us to capture them, change the locks, and use them for Him. Satan's fortresses must be torn down.

We also need to pull down those lofty partitions (v. 5). These include "speculations," those rebel thoughts that take us far away from the knowledge of God. We must say, "This thought is from the devil. I judge it in the name of Jesus Christ. Partition, come down."

Friend, you are not responsible for every thought that flashes into your mind. Satan can plant thoughts in our minds. But you are responsible for what you do with them once they are there. Our job is to recognize and dismiss evil thoughts. That's the idea behind Paul's statement about "taking every thought captive to the obedience of Christ" (2 Cor. 10:5). This is war language. When the enemy sends us one of his thoughts, we need to grab that thought and take it hostage.

We can do this by telling ourselves, "This thought is not like God's thoughts. It is against God and His revealed will. No matter how positively this thought makes me feel, or no matter how anxious it makes me feel—no matter how much I may want to act on it or worry about it—it's a thought out of hell, sent from the enemy. In Christ's authority, I am going to make it my captive and dismiss it." When we can do this successfully day in and day out, we are going to start winning some serious spiritual victories, because whoever controls the mind controls the battle. When you start taking all those roaming enemy thoughts captive, Satan no longer has any influence over you, and you are operating with the mind of Christ.

And while not all anxiety is purely a spiritual matter—because for some, anxiety is the result of imbalanced chemicals in the body or rooted in past traumas which produce triggers—this approach toward overcoming anxious thoughts can help to reduce anxiety. It may not remove anxiety entirely if a person struggles with physical-based symptoms, but it can provide a way to manage it. But in order to do so, you have to take each thought captive to Christ. No army can afford to have enemy troops running around loose behind its lines, wreaking havoc, and sabotaging its weapons and defenses. You may be thinking, *Tony, this sounds too easy.* If you have been a spiritual POW for very long, you may think Satan's strongholds are too hard to conquer. You may think the battle is hopeless, the problems too great. But this is one reason we have so many problems. We make the Christian life harder than God makes it. Yes, there are difficult problems. I don't want to minimize that. But many of the problems we're facing are not as difficult as we make them, because we approach them with a defeatist attitude.

What is the difference between a person God delivers in twenty-four hours and a person who takes twenty-four years to get free? In most cases, I believe, the difference is in the mind. When the thinking changes, the actions change. And then the fortress comes down.

Let me give you an example of how this works. Joshua

and the army of Israel came to the city of Jericho, which was surrounded by a high wall (Joshua 6). It looked impregnable. It was a fortress. God told Israel to march around the city for six days, and then march around it seven times on the seventh day. Then the priests were to blow the trumpets, the people were to shout, and the wall would fall down. Imagine Joshua saying, "Excuse me, Lord, but this is a war. These people are the enemy. They are strong. Would You please give me my military instructions?"

Joshua didn't do that, of course. He obeyed God, and when the priests blew the trumpets and the people shouted, that wall crashed down instantly. The wall fell because the people tore it down God's way. If they had used human methods, they would have been defeated.

This is the question we always face: Are we going to use human or divine methods? It saves a lot of time and grief to use God's method. By looking at the book of James, let's see what's involved in His method for countering Satan's attack on our minds.

COME TO GOD IN FAITH

The apostle James has solid advice for us when we are facing a difficulty in life. If you need wisdom for your problem, James simply says, ask God (1:5). But you need to ask a certain way:

> [Let him] ask in faith without any doubting, for the one who doubts is like the surf of the sea, driven and tossed

by the wind. For that man ought not to expect that he will receive anything from the Lord, being a double-minded man, unstable in all his ways. (vv. 6–8)

The double-minded person, who is trying to operate from a human and divine viewpoint at the same time, knows what everybody else thinks and what God says, and is trying to entertain both views. That kind of person won't receive the answer he needs from God. You're wasting your time if you are trying to mix and match God's way with man's way.

GO TO THE ROOT

If we are going to counter Satan's attack with an offensive of our own, we need to address the root cause of the problem we're facing, not just its symptoms. The root cause is not what someone is doing. A person may say, "I have a drug problem." No, you have a drug symptom. "I have a moral problem." No, you have a moral symptom. "I have an alcohol problem." No, you have an alcohol symptom. The symptom is what you do. The root is the thinking that makes you do it.

James says, "Draw near to God and He will draw near to you. Cleanse your hands, you sinners; and purify your hearts, you double-minded" (James 4:8). There are two things to do here. Cleansing the hands refers to confessing and getting rid of the wrong things we are doing. But notice that James goes beyond the hands to the heart. We must purify our hearts, because if we merely stop doing wrong things without dealing with the internal problem that caused the wrong behavior, we will soon go back to the wrong behavior. This is why so many people's New Year's resolutions fail and why so many Christians' good intentions never get fulfilled. What they are doing is not the main problem. They need to fix the root that is producing the fruit.

SEE SIN GOD'S WAY

How, then, do we deal with the real problem? How do we fix our thinking? How do we cleanse our hearts? James answers that in James 4:9–10. He says, "Be miserable and mourn and weep; let your laughter be turned into mourning and your joy to gloom. Humble yourselves in the presence of the Lord, and He will exalt you."

A lot of people misinterpret the promise at the end of verse 10. James is not saying that God will exalt you to some high position in society. He is saying that God will exalt you above your problem, above that which is keeping you down and making you a spiritual POW. But before God can lift us up, He has to take us low. God wants us to weep and mourn over our sin. He wants us to start seeing our sin the way He sees it. When we do that, then we'll get the help that God gives.

But that help won't come as long as we are lighthearted about sin. Satan's goal is to get us to laugh and joke about sin, to take it lightly so we don't do anything about it. James says we ought to be mourning over our sin, not laughing. We ought to be crying in the presence of a holy God. It's time to take the offensive against sin, confessing, "Lord, this is not just a problem; this is sin. This is not simply a bad habit; it's rebellion against your holiness. This is not just something that everybody does; it's something I shouldn't be doing."

When we begin to see sin the way God sees it, then we will experience what the psalmist meant when he said, "The Lord is near to the brokenhearted and saves those who are crushed in spirit" (Ps. 34:18; see also Ps. 51:17). The Lord says in Isaiah 66:2, "To this one I will look, to him who is humble and contrite of spirit, and who trembles at My word."

Aligning yourself—including your thoughts and actions—underneath the rule of God positions you to live out the victory Christ secured for you on the cross. A warrior who goes against the commands and direction of the person in charge of the battle will never be on the winning side of the war. It is only in humbling yourself beneath the comprehensive rule of God that you strengthen yourself for the battle.

4

Satan's Character and Strategy

We've looked at the pride and rebellion of Satan, how he went from being the anointed cherub of God to the archenemy of God. We've also discussed the way in which Satan carried his battle against God from heaven to earth, bringing with him one third of the angels when God banished him to this planet. Now that we have looked at the battlefield and identified the combatants, we need to study our enemy and his forces in more detail before we move on to the resources God has given us for spiritual warfare. So for the next two chapters, I want to look at the character and strategy of Satan, and at the nature and activity of his demons. But we will not focus solely on our enemy. We will also consider the pivotal point in this great cosmic battle—Satan's defeat at the hands of Jesus Christ.

THE CHARACTER OF SATAN

Satan's evil character was formed the moment he let his pride cause him to rebel against the throne of God. This creature went from a beautiful, flawless being named Lucifer, living in the light and glory of heaven, to Satan the prince of darkness, banished to the earth. And Jesus said that he fell from heaven "like lightning" (Luke 10:18). This is one of many Bible passages that speak of Satan's judgment by God and the curse imposed on him. His curse was evident in his change of name and change of destination.

We know that before his fall, this angel's name was Lucifer (Isa. 14:12 KJV). But in Luke 10:18 Jesus called him Satan. People's names were very important in the Bible because names reflected character. The names of God reflect God's character. The name given to Christ's followers at Antioch, "Christians" (Acts 11:26), reflected their conversion and allegiance to Him. The names given to Lucifer after his fall reflect his character. "Satan" is one of those names. It means "adversary" or "opposer." His curse is revealed in the fact that he went from Lucifer, meaning "shining one," to a name meaning "adversary," the one who opposes everyone and everything associated with God.

When you rebel against God, it will always affect your character. That's why being right with God is so important. Satan's character was corrupted so completely that God gave him a different name. Lucifer had lost his brilliance and righteousness, so he got a name that reflected his fallen status.

Actually, the Bible has multiple names for our enemy.

Satan, used over fifty times in the New Testament, is one name we are very familiar with. Another is the devil, which is used over thirty times in the New Testament, and means "accuser" or "slanderer." The devil is the great accuser of God's people. That's why the saints rejoice when he is finally "thrown down" by God (Rev. 12:9).

The devil's nature is revealed in the great contest of Job 1–2. By accusing Job of serving God for gain, Satan was slandering both Job's character and God's character. Remember, everything our enemy does is ultimately directed at God. The devil hates God and wants to do anything he can to injure God's reputation so that He doesn't get the glory due to Him. But because the devil can't touch God, he seeks to destroy God's glory by attacking His people. This is why the devil is regularly in God's presence, accusing and slandering the saints. The idea of an accuser suggests a legal setting, a court scene. We need to understand that God operates His universe like a court. He gave Israel His law, and throughout the Old Testament, we find God bringing a charge against His people when they broke that law.

Lucifer himself was brought into the court of heaven, charged with rebellion, found guilty, and sentenced to the lake of fire. His fellow rebellious angels were also sentenced to eternal fire. Now the devil is on death row, even though he is being allowed to operate for a period of time. He has taken the role of prosecutor, bringing charges against us before God, accusing us, slandering us and God.

To be effective, an accuser needs an opportunity to make an accusation. He needs something he can try to pin on the person being accused. Paul urges us, "Do not give the devil an opportunity" to accuse us (Eph. 4:27). Paul chose the right name for the enemy here, because the devil is the accuser or slanderer who seeks to tie us up with guilt. When we give the devil an opportunity, an opening—in this case in Ephesians 4, by letting our anger get out of control—then at that point, he has a legal right to accuse us before God. The devil knows what kind of Judge God is and how His court works. He knows that God is so righteous and holy that He has to deal with sin. So when we sin, we give the devil the opportunity he wants to go into God's courtroom and lay a charge against us.

Satan cannot touch our salvation. But he is always ready to take advantage of our sin to ruin our lives. This is so important because God's justice demands that He always deal with sin. When we as believers sin, we damage our fellowship with God and give the devil an open door to operate in our lives. This is why the Bible urges us to deal decisively with sin (1 John 1:9). If we don't, the devil turns that opportunity for accusation into a fortress. And when we allow him to build a fortress, we're in trouble, because the devil now has undue influence over us. Don't let him bring you under his accusing control. Thankfully, we have a "defense attorney," Jesus Christ, to defend us by pleading His blood (1 John 2:1).

The Bible has many other descriptive names and designations for Satan. For example, he is called "the god of this world" (2 Cor. 4:4) and "the prince of the power of the air" (Eph. 2:2) because right now, he's in control of this planet.

Satan has demonized this world. And Jesus tells us, "The thief comes only to steal and kill and destroy" (John 10:10). He is a thief who wants to steal your joy, your effectiveness for Christ, and anything else he can take from you. He is a killer, "a murderer from the beginning" (John 8:44). Because of Satan, Adam and Eve died. Because of Satan, Cain killed Abel. And because of Satan, all the children of Adam will die someday. Satan would kill you and me if possible. He is a destroyer who wants to wreck everything and everyone God has made.

Revelation 12:1–9 also gives us information about our enemy's names, character, and activity. In verse 3, the devil is called the "great red dragon" (this is where people get the idea that Satan wears a red jumpsuit). He is then repeatedly referred to as a dragon in the following verses. And notice that John also calls the devil "the serpent of old" (v. 9), a reference to his deception in the Garden of Eden. A dragon is basically a serpent on steroids. A dragon is a destructive creature, like the ones portrayed in films. A dragon may be mythical and not an actual being, but the Bible draws on the imagery of a terrifying, destructive beast to characterize Satan. He is a destructive creature who can likewise appear like an angel of light (2 Cor. 11:14), manipulating you through the alluring pull of desire.

Did you know that the devil can give you a lot of stuff? He can because this world has been "handed over" to him temporarily. Scripture says that "the whole world lies in the power of the evil one" (1 John 5:19). And as the devil told Jesus in His temptation, "I give it to whomever I wish" (Luke

4:6). Satan can give people power, wealth, friends, and fun on a mammoth scale. So Satan can do you some earthly good. But when he does, he has something bad in mind. It's sort of like those letters you get in the mail from credit card companies, congratulating you on your "outstanding credit history" and making you feel special because you have been hand-selected from among the masses to receive one of their cards with a high dollar limit. These letters actually make you think you have accomplished something and deserve a reward. But credit card companies are not out to do you a favor. They have one overriding concern: to collect from you. The buying power they want to give you comes with a high price.

I'm not trying to equate credit card companies with the devil. But a similar principle is at work. Satan can give you "buying power," but he'll be there to collect heavy interest when the bill comes due. And the interest he seeks to collect is your destruction. Everything Satan does is wrapped up in lies, because deception is at the heart of everything he does. Jesus said concerning the devil, "He . . . does not stand in the truth because there is no truth in him. Whenever he speaks a lie, he speaks from his own nature, for he is a liar and the father of lies" (John 8:44).

How many times have you ordered something online that looked like just what you wanted, but when the product arrives, it doesn't look nearly as good as it did online? Satan knows how to put together an alluring array of temptations. But Jesus said that Satan is incapable of doing anything but lying. He is so thoroughly corrupt that lies are the bone and sinew of his nature. Satan is the ultimate deceiver and manipulator. He will either make a promise that he doesn't deliver on, or he won't tell you the whole story. When the thing gets delivered, you find out it isn't what you thought it was, and you don't like what you're getting. In fact, Jesus called the devil the "father of lies" because he gave birth to deception. He told the first lie to the angels who followed him in his rebellion. He continued lying in the Garden of Eden, and he has been at it ever since. He's out to deceive the whole world (Rev. 12:9). And the people he controls are his deceivers too (2 John 7).

If Satan is the father of lies, that means he has a family. Jesus prefaced His statement about the devil in John 8:44 by saying to the Jewish religious leaders, "You are of your father the devil, and you want to do the desires of your father." We aren't the judge of people's hearts, but Jesus said that many people who call Him "Lord" will not enter heaven (Matt. 7:21). Why? Because they have been deceived by the devil into substituting their self-righteousness for God's righteousness.

If Satan cannot get you to believe his lies or fall into one of his traps, he will turn around and oppose and resist anything you try to do for God. You can bank on Satan's opposition in your efforts to live for Christ, but that's a good sign because it means that Satan considers you worth opposing! He doesn't waste his time messing around with people who aren't doing anything. People who never feel the devil's opposition probably aren't doing much for God. The devil knows he can't touch you and me in terms of condemning us to hell, so he is content to let us go our way as long as we don't try to invade his kingdom and make an impact for Christ. But when we get serious about serving God, the adversary shows up. He's not about to stand by and let us plunder his kingdom. Remember, he's still determined to steal God's glory, so he's going to oppose anything that brings God glory.

It all comes back to the fact that we are in a war with a powerful enemy. But even soldiers in a war are given times of what is called R & R, "rest and recuperation" leave. How do we get some R & R from Satan? By praising God. In fact, the stronger the opposition, the more you need to praise God in the midst of your opposition. Satan can't handle praise. He's allergic to worship. He has to flee because when we praise God, He shows up to enjoy our praises. And Satan cannot abide in the presence of God. So if your adversary is opposing you hard right now, it's time to praise! When you praise, you resist Satan's opposition (see James 4:7).

THE STRATEGY OF SATAN

The story is told of a farmer who was constantly having his watermelons stolen by thieves. The farmer came up with a brilliant idea to thwart the thieves. He poisoned one watermelon, then put a sign in his watermelon field that read: "Warning: One of these watermelons has been poisoned." The next day, the farmer went out to find that none of his melons had been stolen, because the thieves didn't know which one was poisoned. He was quite satisfied that his idea had worked and that he would not have a problem with theft anymore. But two days after the farmer put up his sign, he came out to his field to find that his sign had been altered. Someone had scratched through his message and had written, "Two of these melons have been poisoned." Our farmer friend had to destroy his whole crop because now he didn't know which other melon was poisoned.

That's what it's like dealing with the devil. No matter what you come up with, he can come up with something smarter. No matter what sign you put up, he can change the wording. No matter what strategy you devise, you can't outwit him.

Satan has a definite strategy, and it can be understood in one word: deception. Satan's strategy for your life and mine is to deceive us. The reason Satan has turned to deception is that he cannot outpower God. Satan tried to overcome God in heaven, and he failed. Satan will never be a match for God. Satan cannot create anything. All he can do is manipulate and maneuver what has been created. Since he cannot match God's power, Satan has to maximize the power he has, and deception is his strong suit.

In 2 Thessalonians 2, Paul is correcting misconceptions about the Day of the Lord:

Let no one in any way deceive you, for it will not come unless the apostasy comes first, and the man of lawlessness is revealed, the son of destruction, who opposes and exalts himself above every so-called god or object of worship, so that he takes his seat in the temple of God, displaying himself as being God. (vv. 3–4)

Paul then says that this "lawless one," the Antichrist, will not be revealed until God's restraint is removed. Then, "that lawless one will be revealed . . . the one whose coming is in accord with the activity of Satan, with all power and signs and false wonders, and with all the deception of wickedness for those who perish" (vv. 8–10).

The appearance of the Antichrist will be Satan's crowning achievement in his plan to deceive the world. The Antichrist will be empowered by Satan, who will give this person great power to pull off the master deception. The "lawless one" will be so powerful that he will sit in the temple as God, and unsaved people will think he is God.

But we don't have to wait until the end times to see the power of Satan at work. Where does Satan get the power he wields over people? From what I call his constitutional superiority over any man or woman. By "constitutional superiority," I mean that Satan is an angel, a spirit being. He does not have the limitations of flesh and blood. Therefore, you and I can't compete with the devil in our own strength. We can't outsmart the master deceiver. He has authority by virtue of his nature. Satan's authority is given by God and limited by God, but it is still a greater authority than you and I exercise.

Satan is also powerful by virtue of his vast experience. He has untold years of experience at being the devil. You aren't the first human he's come against. He has been against smarter and stronger people than you and me, and he has won. One thing Satan has learned during all these years is how to transform himself, as we saw earlier in 2 Corinthians 11:14. He can make himself look like one of the good guys.

He is the master chameleon as well as the master deceiver. He can become any color he needs to be to pull off his lie. He seeks to camouflage himself and his plans. Satan is so good and so experienced at deception that the Bible says one day he will deceive all the nations of the world (Rev. 20:8). This world is a puppet, and Satan holds the strings.

Another reason that Satan is so powerful in carrying out his strategy is that he commands a massive organization of evil (see Eph. 6:12). Satan's organization is well run and heavily disguised. Our enemy has a well-laid-out program to deceive and destroy. We need to look at the process of his deceptive strategy, how it actually works, and what it leads to. It occurs in four distinct stages.

Stage One: Desire

The apostle James outlines the process by which Satan deceives people. It begins with desire: "Let no one say when he is tempted, 'I am being tempted by God'; for God cannot be tempted by evil, and He Himself does not tempt anyone. But each one is tempted when he is carried away and enticed by his own lust" (James 1:13–14). Stage one in Satan's plan is the arousal of a desire. Even legitimate desires can become a problem when Satan tempts us to meet a legitimate desire in an illegitimate way. The process of temptation often means trying to get us to meet a good need in a bad way. For example, the desire for food is good, but gluttony is sin. The desire for sex is legitimate, but immorality is sin. The desire for sleep is good, but lying in bed all day is laziness and sin.

Satan knows you can't just jettison your desires because

our desires are God-given. So the enemy wants to control how your desires are met. This is the issue in temptation. Satan wants your desires to master you, rather than you mastering your desires. He wants the desire to take control. It's called addiction.

Stage Two: Deception

In stage two of the process, the illegitimate development of desire leads to deception, the moment when the person takes Satan's bait and finds out he's been deceived. The idea here is of a fisherman. A smart fisherman doesn't just throw a bare hook in the water and wait. The hook has to be covered with some kind of bait for a fish to bite on it and get caught.

Satan is not just throwing bare hooks out in front of us. He doesn't say to a man, "Come on down to the local bar and let me get you addicted to alcohol so you can lose your job and your family, lose your self-respect and self-control, and wind up in a rehab center." Satan is far too smart to let his hooks show. He covers them with enticing bait. He invites a person down to the friendly neighborhood tavern for one drink, then two, three, and four, until that person's desire for alcohol overcomes all his other desires and commitments. He has been thoroughly deceived.

Satan deceives us by planting an evil thought or idea in our minds. He can't make us do anything, but he can build deceitful castles of desire in our minds. King David found that out. Look at what happened when he saw Bathsheba bathing. He could have turned away, but Satan got him to keep looking and then thinking and then acting. The Bible says that on another occasion in David's life, "Satan stood up against Israel and moved David to number Israel" (1 Chron. 21:1). David got the idea, "I don't need God. I have a big enough army to take care of it myself." But seventy thousand people died because of David's sin.

Peter asked Ananias, "Why has Satan filled your heart to lie to the Holy Spirit?" about the money Ananias and Sapphira had received from the sale of their land (Acts 5:3). This couple's desire to sell their land and give the money to the church in Jerusalem was legitimate. And the money they earned from the sale was legitimate income. If they had just given a certain amount and been honest about it, there would have been no problem. But Satan tempted them to twist their story and say they had given it all when they had not, and they died.

Satan knows how to intertwine our desires with his twisted plans to lure us into his deception. But we still have to bite on the hook.

Stage Three: Disobedience

Desire leads to deception, and deception leads to disobedience. "When lust has conceived, it gives birth to sin" (James 1:15). James uses the analogy of conception, pregnancy, and birth because the birth process so closely parallels the process he is talking about. When an illegitimate desire is welcomed and acted upon, that act of conception produces a "child" called sin. And once a child has been conceived, its birth is sure to follow. In other words, committing disobedience is like the act of procreation. The result will always show up after a while. The child of disobedience is sin, and like any other child, sin will begin to grow once it has been born.

Part of becoming mature in Christ, as opposed to becoming grown-up children of sin, is learning to submit our feelings to the will of Christ, to operate on the basis of what we know to be true rather than just what we feel. But sin will keep you spiritually immature, a slave to your emotions.

But let us keep in mind Philippians 2:13: "It is God who is at work in you, both to will and to work for His good pleasure." When your will is combined with God's will, He gives you the power to do what your will is telling you you ought to do. You are not fighting this battle alone. You have tremendous power available to you in Christ.

Stage Four: Death

The fourth and final stage in Satan's process is death. James says, "When sin is accomplished, it brings forth death" (1:15). Sin certainly brings spiritual death. That is one of the fundamental truths we learn from the sin of Adam and Eve. Sin can also produce physical death, as we saw in the previous section.

Satan brings nothing but death and destruction with him, but God is the source of "every perfect gift" (1:17). So James says, "Do not be deceived, my beloved brethren" (v. 16). When Satan deceives and leads us into sin, he causes us to miss the goodness of God. Don't ever think you have it better with Satan than you do with God. Satan wants us to roll his ideas over in our minds, to play with them until we start feeling better about them. But that's a process that will lead to death if we follow it, so we must resist. Jesus is our perfect example here. When confronted by Satan's temptations in the wilderness, Jesus did not say, "Let Me think about it, and I'll get back to you later." He said, "It is written." He dealt with the temptation on the spot, right in Satan's face. He didn't meditate upon the wrong desires Satan suggested and allow them to conceive disobedience.

When it comes to believers, one of Satan's purposes is to interrupt the process by which God gets glory through our lives. He wants to render us ineffective in terms of any real impact for Christ. That's why he keeps some believers depressed, some discouraged, and others underneath their circumstances. Satan has two primary reasons for using his deceptive strategy on you. First, he wants to disarm you emotionally, spiritually, and physically because he knows you can do nothing for God if you're miserable. God won't get glory if you're too miserable to give it to Him. In fact, Satan can twist things so much that he'll get you blaming God for your misery. And if you're not careful, the devil can wind up using you to bring unhappiness and misery to others. He will use us to be his deceivers if we let him.

Second, the devil wants to prevent you and me from accomplishing the will of God by frustrating God's will for our lives. Satan even tried to frustrate the accomplishment of God's will in Jesus' life. God the Father's will for His Son was the cross, but in the wilderness temptation, the devil tried to get Jesus to take the easy way. Satan also used one of Jesus' own disciples to try to turn Him away from the cross

(Matt. 16:21–22). Imagine Peter rebuking Jesus, trying to tell Him that He was wrong. Only Satan could have thought of an attack that bold. Jesus knew who was behind it, and He told Peter, "Get behind Me, Satan!" (v. 23). Jesus was basically saying, "Get behind Me, devil. I have to go to the cross. Peter, Satan is using you, one of My children, to stop Me from doing My Father's will."

If Satan wasn't afraid to try to turn Jesus away from God's will in going to the cross, do you think he will leave us alone? Of course not. As a matter of fact, Jesus went on to say in this same passage, "If anyone wishes to come after Me, he must deny himself, and take up his cross and follow Me" (v. 24). Satan tried to get Jesus to focus on the suffering of the cross and thus to avoid it. Our enemy will do the same to us.

Let's face it. The cross does involve suffering. It's an instrument of death. Bearing my cross means I am willing to identify publicly with Jesus Christ and accept anything that goes with that identification. It means I will bear the scars of being identified with Christ. You say, "But that can be hard." Only if you don't see the resurrection that follows crucifixion. Ask any Olympic athlete if it's hard preparing for the games. Ask him or her if there is any pain or suffering involved in four years of training. But then ask the winner of an Olympic gold medal how it feels to stand on that platform and receive that medal. He or she will tell you all the pain and hardship was worth it.

You and I are going to experience some tough times in following Christ. Satan is looking to attack us on all sides. But when we step onto the winner's stand and receive the crown from Jesus Christ, we will say, "It was worth it." Don't let Satan deceive and distract you from accomplishing God's will as a true warrior of the King.

5

The Nature and Activity of Demons

One of the fundamental truths of spiritual warfare is that Satan isn't operating alone. He has his own army of spirit beings called demons who obey him and carry out his agenda. A demon is a fallen angel who followed Satan in his rebellion (see Rev. 12:4) and now assists Satan's program of opposition to God's purpose, program, and people. The existence of demons has generally been either denied or caricatured by the world. Hollywood has always been fascinated by the demonic, and many popular movies feature demon-like forces or aliens bent on destroying the earth.

But the Bible's teaching about the true nature and purpose of demons has been largely rejected by the world and even by many theologians and preachers. This isn't surprising, as Satan himself moves to camouflage himself so that people don't know he's there.

The Bible is clear that demons are real, and we need to

understand their operation and purposes. We don't need to fear demons, but because they are active troops in Satan's army, we need to know more about them so we can be more alert and experience greater success in spiritual warfare. The Bible says that God created countless hosts of angels. Since one third of the angels followed Satan in his rebellion and were judged with him, you can imagine the vast array of demons Satan has at his command.

According to Matthew 12:24–26, demons are part of Satan's kingdom—and notice that Jesus says there is no division in that realm. Satan is not about to cast out Satan. This is important to understand. One reason that Satan's demonic regime is so successful and powerful is because it is so unified. There are no "Benedict Arnold" demons. These beings have been forever confirmed in unrighteousness, just as the good angels who did not follow Satan have been forever confirmed in holiness. No demon gets up in the morning and says, "I don't feel like being a demon today. I want to repent and turn back to God." Demons are loyal to their evil leader, Satan.

THE NATURE OF DEMONS

The well-known story of Jesus' encounter with the demon-possessed man in Luke 8:26–39 tells us pretty much all we need to know about the nature of demons:

> [Jesus] was met by a man from the city who was pos-
> sessed with demons; and who had not put on any

clothing for a long time, and was not living in a house, but in the tombs. Seeing Jesus, he cried out and fell before Him, and said in a loud voice, "What business do we have with each other, Jesus, Son of the Most High God? I beg You, do not torment me." (vv. 27–28)

This man was demon-possessed, or "demonized," which is a better translation of the Greek term used here and throughout the Gospels. When Jesus showed up, this man fell to the ground and cried out, asking Jesus not to torment him. Why? Because Jesus and demons can't be in the same place at the same time and get along. Somebody has to move when Jesus shows up. As we examine this account, we learn some important things about the nature of demons.

First, demons are personal beings—that is, they display the primary attributes of personality. For example, demons possess intellect. In this story, they recognized Jesus and were able to speak and reason using this man's voice (v. 28).

Second, demons have emotions. They begged Jesus not to torment them (v. 28). Since demons do not have bodies of their own, the torment they feel would apparently be in the spiritual or emotional realm.

Third, demons have a will. In verses 32–33, they expressed their desire to enter into the herd of pigs that was feeding nearby. We also know that demons have a will because they exercised that will when they chose to follow Satan in his rebellion. So it's not surprising that they were able to make a choice here. But note that they had no power to do what they wanted to do without Christ's permission.

When we see people committing evil, strange, or destructive acts, the usual assumption is that they are insane or mentally unbalanced. The demoniac of Luke 8 certainly appeared to be insane, even dangerously insane. Living among graves without clothes is a crazy thing to do. But in reality, he was possessed, not just insane. That's why when we are dealing with people who have certain emotional, mental, or spiritual problems, we must consider whether a demonic influence is being exerted on that individual. If we are dealing with a serious spiritual warfare issue and it's unaddressed, then we will never be able to fix what's wrong.

The personal nature of demons is important because they are often portrayed on television shows or in films either as some sort of impersonal evil force or as something make-believe to be dismissed. It's part of Satan's deception to cause people not to take him or his henchmen seriously.

Yet demons are not only personal beings. They are also spirit beings. Paul says specifically that our struggle is "not against flesh and blood" (Eph. 6:12). Demons do not have bodies of their own, but as we saw above, they are able to inhabit the bodies of others.

Jesus revealed more about the nature of demons when He said,

> When the unclean spirit goes out of a man, it passes through waterless places seeking rest, and not finding any, it says, "I will return to my house from which I came." And when it comes, it finds it swept and put in order. Then it goes and takes along seven other spirits

more evil than itself, and they go in and live there; and
the last state of that man becomes worse than the first.
(Luke 11:24–26)

It was important for a person who faced demonic powers
bent on his destruction, as well as the nation of Israel, to
make the right decision about Jesus as Messiah, or he would
soon be in a worse spiritual condition than when he started.

Notice what Jesus said about demons in the course of His
teaching. They are restless when they have no one through
whom to express themselves. "Waterless places" are places
without life. Like the demons who inhabited the man in
Luke 8, this demon became frustrated when it had no way to
express itself, so it returned to the place of its former habita-
tion—and it brought the brotherhood!

The demon called this man's body "my house" (Luke
11:24). In Jesus' illustration, the demon returned and had a
"family reunion" at the man's expense. Demons often seek a
"house" to inhabit in order to find temporary peace and not
be sent to the abyss. They are spirit beings who can use the
bodies of humans and animals to express themselves.

The demons of hell are powerful beings. The demons
who possessed the man Jesus healed in Luke 8 were forc-
ing him to do violent things, and they gave him superhuman
strength. He could break chains as if they were string. No
doubt, the demons would have eventually killed him, since
demons can even drive people to want to commit suicide
(Rev. 9:3–6).

Many cases are recorded of people on drugs having so much strength that it takes a small army of people to restrain them. That's likely not just the chemical in the drug working on them. Drugs and sorcery or witchcraft of any kind are vehicles for demonic activity.

Demons are also perverted beings. When they rejected God and lined up with Satan, they "earned" a special name. Not only are they called demons, but Jesus called them "unclean spirits." They pervert everything they touch. As we will see in more detail later, demons pervert the truth of God (1 Tim. 4:1). They want you and me to believe a lie because their leader, Satan, is the father of lies. Paul says they want to pervert God's goodness and the good things God created. That's why John tells us to "test the spirits" (1 John 4:1). Testing the spirits means knowing which ones are exalting Jesus and which are not, because that's always the test. Demons can't handle the presence of Christ. They can't handle the cross or the blood of Christ, or anything that has to do with Him. They leave when Christ is exalted.

Demons are also eager to pervert human sexual relationships (see 1 Cor. 7:5; Rev. 18:2–3). Sometimes they have even been able to mix perversion with religious devotion, as in the worship of Aphrodite practiced in Corinth. Demons are perverted, but the problem is they don't always appear to be so. They want to make their perversion as attractive as possible, even using a twisted version of God's Word against people. That's why you must always measure what you hear by the Word, not by how well it was said or the fact that the person saying it was holding a Bible.

THE ACTIVITIES OF DEMONS

The Bible reveals two basic categories of demons: those who are not yet permanently judged and are free to move about doing Satan's will, and a subclass of demons who were imprisoned for their particular sin.

The first category of demons is the one we are most familiar with, those demons who are free to move about at Satan's bidding and carry out his purposes. When I say they are free, I'm using that term in a relative sense. Demons are under the ultimate control of heaven, as Jesus made clear on a number of occasions when He told demons what to do and they had to obey. In Luke 8, the demons that Christ cast out of the man not only had to leave him when Jesus commanded them to, but they had to ask Jesus' permission to go into the pigs. But since God has chosen to let these "free" demons operate for the time being, they are able to carry out Satan's commands.

Even in this we can see a reminder that Satan is not the equal of God. Satan can't be everywhere at the same time, he doesn't know everything, and he's not all-powerful. So he needs the demons as his agents to carry out his will. The difference is that God uses His angels by choice, not out of necessity.

In Luke 8, the demons inhabiting this man begged Jesus "not to command them to go away into the abyss" (v. 31). This is the place where all demons that are active now will ultimately be sent (see Rev. 9:1). But these demons were worried that Jesus would send them there ahead of their time, we might say, so that they would be out of commission. Jesus did not send them to the abyss, of course, but allowed them to enter the pigs. There's no record in Scripture of Jesus consigning an active demon to this prison during His earthly ministry. But the demons knew that Jesus had the power to order them to the abyss, and they were worried.

It's like the game of dodgeball. Once you get hit with the ball, you lose, and you're out of the game. You're active until you are hit, and then that's it. The demons knew that anytime Jesus showed up, He had the prerogative to take them out of the game permanently. They didn't want that, and they never doubted Jesus' power to do it. We don't need to doubt Jesus' power over hell either.

The Bible refers to a second group of demons, those who are permanently imprisoned because of the exceptionally gross nature of their sin. According to Jude 6, these angels "did not keep their own domain, but abandoned their proper abode." They are being "kept in eternal bonds under darkness for the judgment of the great day." Peter writes of these demons that "God did not spare angels when they sinned, but cast them into hell and committed them to pits of darkness, reserved for judgment" (2 Peter 2:4).

What is the "proper abode" of angels? Heavenly places, the spiritual realm. These angels left that sphere when they came down to earth to commit an especially wicked sin. We referred to that sin earlier, the time when these angels cohabited with women and produced a mutant race of giants (Gen. 6:1–4). This was Satan's race that he hoped would take over. But God found a faithful man in Noah, defeated Satan, and destroyed this evil race of men. For leaving their proper abode after creation and committing that sin, these angels were cast into eternal judgment, locked up with no possibility of release or parole forever.

THE GOAL OF DEMONS

To Promote Satan

We can state the goal of hell in one simple sentence: The goal of hell, the demonic agenda, is to promote who Satan is and what he does, and to oppose everything that God is and does. This is the essence of spiritual warfare.

In promoting Satan's agenda, demons promote his doctrine. They teach what their master wants taught so people might live in the darkness of lies rather than in the light of God's truth.

In 1 Timothy 4, Paul talks about "deceitful spirits and doctrines of demons" (v. 1) and says that in the end times, people will pay closer and closer attention to these teachings. One particular doctrine that demons propagate is the idea that God is not good (vv. 3–4). This ought to sound familiar, because this was the argument of the devil back in Eden. Satan was essentially saying to Eve, "If God were good, He wouldn't keep you away from that tree. He would share it with you." Satan wants you to believe God is holding out on you. But we know from Scripture that if God is withholding something from you, it's because what you want isn't good for you. You may say, "But it looks good. It tastes good. It feels good." These are not the proper criteria, however, because things that look and taste and feel good can actually be bad.

Demonic doctrine hits at things God created to be enjoyed, such as marriage and food (v. 3). To appreciate this, you have to understand that in Paul's day there was a view that divided nature between spirit and matter. Things that were associated with matter, such as the body, were viewed as evil. Things that were associated with the spirit were viewed as good. This was a false dichotomy and a false view of spirituality.

But those who know the truth know that God has not forbidden marriage or the eating of certain foods. Instead, He has created these things to "be gratefully shared in" (v. 3) by His people. Then notice what Paul said. "For everything created by God is good, and nothing is to be rejected if it is received with gratitude" (v. 4). The problem was that false teachers under the influence of demons were keeping the Christians in Timothy's charge from enjoying what God had provided for them. These teachers were promoting spirituality through asceticism.

If your Christian life is all about the negatives, if your spirituality is measured only in can'ts and don'ts, then you've been duped by demons—in some form or another. If you live your Christian life with ingratitude, if you only look at what you don't have or can't have because you're a Christian, then you're missing out on maximizing your spiritual potential.

Paul calls it a doctrine of demons that limits the Christian life to an experience of negatives. Don't get me wrong.

There are things we can't do as believers, but these prohibitions are not the essence of Christianity. God has given us all things to enjoy (see 1 Tim. 6:17). Satan and his demons want to point out the one tree you can't eat from rather than the thousand trees you can enjoy.

How do you know whether something is from God? When you can authenticate it by the Word and pray over it legitimately (1 Tim. 4:5). Those are the two criteria to determine whether something is from God.

Demonic doctrine wants to not only distract you from God's goodness, but also undermine the Son of God. In another familiar passage, Paul warned the Corinthians that the adversary wanted to undercut their devotion to Christ (2 Cor. 11:3). Demons want to remove Christ from the center of your life. They know that as long as Christ is at the center, they cannot have dominance over you. Demons want to discredit and steal away the work of Christ in your heart and mine, so that we would become distracted and sidetracked.

Demons are also working hard to undermine the gospel of God by blinding people to its truth:

> And even if our gospel is veiled, it is veiled to those who are perishing, in whose case the god of this world has blinded the minds of the unbelieving so that they might not see the light of the gospel of the glory of Christ, who is the image of God. (2 Cor. 4:3–4)

The demonic world wants to put blinders on the unrighteous. If you have ever tried to witness to people who simply couldn't grasp the idea that they can't earn their salvation, or who refused to believe they were sinners, then you know the truth of what the Scripture is saying. The Holy Spirit has to break through that spiritual fog for people to see the goodness of God in His gospel.

Jesus said the devil is in the business of destroying everyone and everything he can (John 10:10). All through the New Testament, we see demonic forces at work to debilitate and destroy people. I'm not saying that all illnesses and other serious problems are demonically orchestrated. However, more physical and emotional illness is demonically orchestrated and influenced than most people are willing to admit. For example, demons can cause blindness (Matt. 12:22), physical deformity (Luke 13:11), emotional and mental instability (Matt. 17:14–18), and even physical death (Rev. 9:13–15). If it were not for the grace of God, any one of us could have been killed before we came to Christ, because total and eternal destruction is Satan's goal.

Even after we come to Christ and the devil loses us for eternity, his program is to destroy our joy and peace, and kill our effectiveness for Christ. And our enemy uses his demons to promote this portion of his evil agenda. Don't forget that Satan is a frustrated ruler. He tried to displace God from the throne of the universe, and he's been out to build his own kingdom ever since. The method he uses is one of seeking to dominate individuals, institutions, and ultimately entire nations. The demons are once again his primary henchmen.

Demons seek to infiltrate and influence organized religion on Satan's behalf. They attempt to bring deceptive teachings and false doctrines into the church to lead God's people astray and keep them from experiencing the work of God in their lives and in their midst (1 Tim. 4:1–5).

Satan ultimately seeks to dominate nations that he might wage war against God and His people. When I was in Israel, I went to "Har-Magedon" (Rev. 16:16), or the Mount of Megiddo, which is located in the valley of Jezreel. This is the place where the Bible says the last great battle between the forces of God and the forces of Satan will be fought (Rev. 19:17–21). God will allow Satan to assemble the leaders of the world's armies at Armageddon in a desperate attempt to wrest control of the universe from Him. But the outcome has already been decided. However, Satan wants dominion so badly that even after one thousand years in bondage during the Millennium, he will lead one last act of rebellion in his final attempt to gain control (Rev. 20:7–9). That will end in his eternal doom. The enemy will never give up seeking to dominate the world until he is finally judged.

Besides pushing Satan's doctrine, destructiveness, and domination, demons are also effective promoters of the devil's distractions. In this category I include all the entertainment programs and psychic hotlines and horoscopes that purport to offer people spiritual guidance and advice. I am convinced that far too many Christians are dabbling in these things and are opening themselves up to the evil spirit world. Satan wants to lure our focus away from Christ by any means possible. I want to be clear about the distractions that demons can bring because the Bible is very clear on this. Let me look at some important passages of Scripture with you.

In Leviticus 19:31, the Mosaic Law warned, "Do not turn to mediums or spiritists; do not seek them out to be defiled by them. I am the Lord your God." In other words, don't visit palm readers or mess with Ouija boards. Don't look to astrology for truth. Don't look into a crystal ball. All that is a denial of the Lord your God. It also makes *you* dirty.

Whenever you appeal to the created order to do what is the Creator's prerogative, you change gods. You are distracted from the true God—and you invite His severe judgment. "As for the person who turns to mediums and to spiritists, to play the harlot after them, I will also set My face against that person and will cut him off from among his people" (Lev. 20:6).

Here's another warning we need to heed: "When you enter the land which the Lord your God gives you, you shall not learn to imitate the detestable things of those nations" (Deut. 18:9). Why? Because "whoever does these things is detestable to the Lord" (v. 12). When you try to add anything to God and do not allow Him to be supreme, you lose His blessing and invite His curse.

At various times in its history, Israel was plagued by false prophets (see Jer. 29:8–9). God always makes a distinction between true and false prophets, because not everybody who uses the name of the Lord is from the Lord (Matt. 7:21–23). Deceivers have always been operating, but now they are getting more sophisticated. The devil's distractions are looking better and better to the gullible. His demons are working hard to divert us from faithfulness to Christ. We don't need to help them by playing around with the things of darkness.

In Acts 19:19, the people who got saved in Ephesus brought all their magic books and burned them. Some of us need to do some "burning" in our houses. We need to get rid of some of the stuff we watch and listen to that promotes divination and magic, either explicitly or implicitly, because these things are compromising God's presence in our homes. We must be able to see through the enemy's distractions.

To Oppose God

Let's go to the second part of the demons' program, which is to oppose the nature and work of God. Demons not only promote hell; they oppose heaven. One of the primary things that demons want to oppose is God's position.

Our God is a jealous God who will not share His glory with any other. He is supreme; we are to have no other gods before Him. So demons seek to oppose God's position primarily through idolatry. In Deuteronomy 32:17, Moses said of Israel's rebellion, "They sacrificed to demons who were not God, to gods whom they have not known, new gods who came lately, whom your fathers did not dread." Watch out for "new gods." There aren't any new gods, just old demons behind the mask of new gods. That's why Moses charged the Israelites with sacrificing to demons when they offered their sacrifices to idols. The people didn't see any demons. They didn't think they were sacrificing to demons. But behind every idol is a demon.

Someone may say, "Well, that's just an Old Testament problem." No, it's a New Testament problem too:

The things which the Gentiles sacrifice, they sacrifice
to demons and not to God; and I do not want you to
become sharers in demons. You cannot drink the cup of
the Lord and the cup of demons; you cannot partake of
the table of the Lord and the table of demons. Or do we
provoke the Lord to jealousy? We are not stronger than
He, are we? (1 Cor. 10:20–22)

Paul was talking about the church at communion, the
table of the Lord, which is designed for intimate fellowship
with the Lord. Paul says that demons have a table set too,
and are enticing believers to sit at it.

How can believers commune at the table of demons?
When we partake of an idol that belongs to the godless,
unbelieving world and let its idols become our idols, we
enter into communion with demons and provoke the Lord
to jealousy.

Some believers may say, "I don't have to worry about
that. I share in the Lord's Table at church, and I don't bow
before any carved images or any stone idols." I'm afraid that
many American Christians dine at two tables. On Sunday,
they dine at the Lord's Table; then on Monday, they dine at
the table of demons, because they have idols in their lives.

An idol is anything that takes the place of God in your
life. Many Christians in this country are bowing before the
idol of materialism. We said above that God has given us
all things to enjoy. There's nothing wrong with you having
things. Materialism is when things have you. That is idolatry.

So the question we need to ask ourselves is, "Am I dining

at two tables?" If the answer is yes, you'd better get it fixed if you want the Lord's fellowship and blessing in your life—and if you want to wage victorious warfare.

The opposition of demons extends to God's purity as well as His position and His precepts. We've talked about the vileness and corruption that Satan and his demons seek to perpetrate. Jude referred to the case of demons who became involved in perverted human sexuality (v. 6), and also referred to the biblical epitome of impurity, Sodom and Gomorrah (v. 7). These cities practiced "gross immorality" and "went after strange flesh."

Then Jude turned to the reason for writing his short letter: the false teachers who were plaguing the church. These men "in the same way . . . defile the flesh" (v. 8). In what manner does Jude mean? In the same manner as the demons and the people of Sodom and Gomorrah.

Demons oppose godly purity. Why? Because the central characteristic of God is His holiness. Demons are really into impurity, and the viler the impurity, the better they like it. They take what's bad and seek to make it even worse.

How do you think it's possible for drug users to keep coming up with new and more harmful drugs? The demons make sure they keep a new batch brewing all the time. Demons are always coming up with something new to promote ungodliness, because with the ungodliness comes the consequences of ungodliness.

All of us have to battle with sin, which is why 1 John 1:9 is so important. We must confess our sins and cleanse ourselves in the blood of Christ, because without His blood, we can't get rid of sin's impurity. And if we can't get rid of the impurity, we can't have fellowship with God. Demons want to keep us defiled and impure, away from the blood. They are unalterably opposed to God's purity.

To Oppose God's People

Here is where the spiritual warfare begins to heat up. Demons stand opposed to God's people—you and me. One way the demonic world opposes us is by slandering us to God. If Satan can use his henchmen to cause us to stumble and fall, then the slanderer has an accusation he can take into heaven's courtroom and fling in God's face. "Did You see what that man just did? Did You hear what that woman said? They claim to be Your children. What are You going to do about it?"

Demons oppose God's people by getting in their way. There are many ways demons can seek to do this. These ways aren't always easily detectable, but they can include things such as demotivating us from following through on God's leading, setting up roadblocks from the direction God has given, or luring us into distractions. Paul said he wanted to come to the Thessalonians, but Satan hindered him (1 Thess. 2:17–18). Some ways are more overt than others.

Demons also oppose us by tempting us to sin. Temptation is still the devil's best weapon against us on a daily basis. He is constantly dropping the seeds of thoughts that later on can produce a messy harvest if we yield to them. And these seeds don't always involve the more notable sins such as lust, perversion, or lying. They can be seeds of pride, jealousy, or anger. Anything that seeks to draw our hearts and minds away from devotion to Christ and following His will is the game plan of demons.

Demons also oppose us by sowing division and discord in the body of Christ. James writes,

> Who among you is wise and understanding? Let him show by his good behavior his deeds in the gentleness of wisdom. But if you have bitter jealousy and selfish ambition in your heart, do not be arrogant and so lie against the truth. This wisdom is not that which comes down from above, but is earthly, natural, *demonic*. For where jealousy and selfish ambition exist, there is disorder and every evil thing. (3:13–16, italics added)

The demons know that God is a God of order and unity, which means He will not operate in a context of disorder and disunity. So they are busy sowing jealousy and selfish ambition in the church and in the home.

If you trace most marital breakups, you will find selfishness lying somewhere at the root. When the church is full of strife and disunity, somewhere in the mess you will usually find someone's ambitions or selfish desires being promoted. Hell loves to see the children of heaven at each other's throats because the enemy knows that when strife shows up, the Holy Spirit is hindered.

Until we are willing to work harder to keep the unity of the Spirit (Eph. 4:3) than we do to promote our interests and our preferences, we will continue to suffer discord in the church and in our homes. Until we get to the point where things don't have to go our way all the time, there will be constant divisions and disorder, and God won't show up. He won't help us.

Demons know what they're doing. They're not a house divided. Their strength is in their unity. They operate as one. If we can learn to operate as one with God, as one in the church, and as one in our homes, there will be no room for demons to work. That's why Paul pleaded, "[Be] diligent to preserve the unity of the Spirit in the bond of peace" (Eph. 4:3). Unity is an indispensable weapon for any warrior.

6

Knowing Our Spiritual Allies

Recently, I met a woman who excitedly showed me her angel pin, a cute little cherub on a pin. Now, I have no problem with someone wanting to wear an angel pin. But when I see how angels are displayed in television shows, porcelain statues, paintings, clothing, earrings or the like, I can't help but reflect on the true biblical nature of angels: awesome, fierce, blazing creatures who inspired fear and trembling whenever they arrived on the scene. Angel pins are nice for jewelry, but they don't do justice to who and what angels truly are.

In the Bible, one of the first things angels always had to say when they appeared was, "Fear not." They are terrifying creatures who surround the throne of God and exist to do His bidding. Angels do so because of a fundamental principle about the nature of God. According to 1 Corinthians 14:33, "God is not a God of confusion." He's a God of order.

So anything that originates from Him must be done "properly and in an orderly manner" (v. 40). Therefore, God's angels, whom God has chosen to assist us in the spiritual battle, must operate in an orderly fashion.

One of Satan's major goals is to bring about confusion, disruption, disharmony, and disorder. He does this because he knows that God will not act in an environment of conflict, chaos, and confusion. For example, the reason Satan wants you and your mate to be fussing and battling each other is that he knows God will not answer a husband's prayers when his attitude toward his wife is not in God's order (1 Peter 3:7).

God steps back from confusion because it contradicts His nature. Rebellion and disorder are antithetical to His very being. His angels operate under His authority because God does everything in an orderly way. Understanding how angels function, what their motivation is, and why God placed them in our lives gives us a greater knowledge on how to better maneuver within the spiritual realm. To increase our understanding of the angelic realm, let's first look at the structure in which they exist.

ORGANIZED BY AUTHORITY

Study of Scripture clearly reveals to us that angels are organized by authority. Paul writes in Colossians 1:16, "For by [Christ] all things were created, both in the heavens and on earth, visible and invisible, whether thrones or dominions or rulers or authorities—all things have been created through Him and for Him." I've read this verse many times over the years, but it wasn't until I came to this study that I noticed several truths important for our understanding of the way God's creation works. First, the fact that Paul talks about Christ creating both earthly and heavenly rulers and authorities underscores a main point we've been making through this book so far: that the activity in the visible world parallels that in the invisible world. For instance, where there's a visible earthly king, spiritual rulers are also operating.

Not only that, but each realm is organized along definite lines of authority. We know that Paul's reference to thrones and dominions alludes to both the angelic and the demonic order because Satan mimics everything God does. God's angels are organized along a clear chain of command. The enemy has his own ranks of demons, too. As the anointed angel, Satan himself used to be at the top of the angelic chain of command. He was the ruler under God of the angelic realm. Then the Bible mentions another anointed angel, the archangel Michael (Jude 9).

There are also the cherubim who are, what we might call, the angelic guard. It was two cherubim who were put at the gate of the Garden of Eden to keep Adam and Eve from returning. Cherubim have a major role to play in protecting the glory of God.

The seraphim are concerned with the holiness and worship of God. We met these awe-inspiring creatures in Isaiah 6. When they worshiped, the whole temple shook. They worship God all day. Another order or tier of angelic beings is the living creatures of Revelation 4. They are unusual creatures engaged in serious worship.

From what we know, this is the angelic order, with each rank of angels functioning under the higher rank. We get a good picture of this angelic order of authority in Revelation 12:7, which describes a war in heaven in which Michael and his angels went to battle against Satan and his angels. Here are two angelic armies, under the authority of their respective leaders, who were squaring off against each other.

Angels are not only organized by authority, but they understand the importance of being under authority. Michael the archangel appreciated the importance of authority. In Jude 9, we see Michael calling on God's authority to deal with Satan: "Michael the archangel, when he disputed with the devil and argued about the body of Moses, did not dare pronounce against him a railing judgment, but said, 'The Lord rebuke you!'" As an archangel, Michael was Satan's counterpart. That's important because most people think God is Satan's counterpart or opposite. No, God has no counterpart. He is the all-powerful Creator. Satan is a created being. If you want to find a counterpart to Satan, look in the angelic world, not at God. God is in a class all by Himself.

Notice that even though Michael is a powerful archangel, he was extremely careful in how he dealt with the devil. Michael knew that Satan had a higher authority than he did.

Michael never forgot who he was, and he never forgot the position Satan once held. So even though they were battling over Moses's body, Michael never tried to leave or usurp his position of authority. He understood that the only way he was going to win his battle against the devil was by invoking the authority of the Lord.

If Michael, the awesome archangel of God, had to be careful in dealing with Satan, how much more careful should you and I be? If you are going to defeat the devil in your life, you are going to need access to God's authority, because you are going to encounter situations where it will take more than the power of positive thinking to deliver you. You're going to need divine intervention, which means you have to be operating under divine authority, just like the angels.

Consider Matthew 8:5, where Jesus comes into Capernaum, a little town off the Sea of Galilee. There He meets a Roman centurion who says, "Lord, my servant is lying paralyzed at home, fearfully tormented." Jesus replies, "I will come and heal him" (vv. 6–7). But notice the centurion's response:

> Lord, I am not worthy for You to come under my roof, but just say the word, and my servant will be healed. For I also am a man under authority, with soldiers under me; and I say to this one, "Go!" and he goes, and to another, "Come!" and he comes, and to my slave, "Do this!" and he does it. (vv. 8–9)

Matthew 8:10 says that Jesus was astounded by the level of this man's faith. This Gentile soldier understood something that many of God's own people in Israel did not—the principle of authority. Because the centurion understood the military chain of authority, he knew that he could appeal to a higher authority, Jesus, to do for him what he asked.

If you need help with a circumstance that's too big for you to handle, you need to invoke the principle of authority.

When you draw on the divine authority you have in Christ, even though you're the one with the problem, it's God's authority that will bring the solution. Jesus says this kind of living takes a kind of faith that few people have. Many times, we go about our day and then ask the Lord to bless it or certain activities, rather than appealing to His authority to intervene and do His work in the situation. This Roman soldier said to Jesus, "If You will just speak the word, my problem will be solved because You have the authority." What the centurion did reflects the way the angels operate. They operate by authority, appealing to the greater to assist the lesser in a problem that is too much for the lesser to handle.

If you're not operating in authority as a way of life, don't suddenly call on God for help when you get in trouble. Many people want convenient authority. They don't want God's authority over them until they need it. This is like a child who wants his parents to come through for him when he's been living an independent life and ignoring their authority. That is a misuse and abuse of authority. The angels understand authority, and that's why Michael invoked God's authority when he faced the devil.

Here's another reality about angels and authority that we need to see: Angels are loyal to their authority figure. This is true both for God's holy angels and for Satan's demons. After the rebellion of Satan, there are no more defections on either side of the angelic world. The angels who followed Satan have already been consigned to eternal condemnation, and the angels who remained true to God were confirmed in righteousness.

Matthew 12 reinforces this. Jesus had cast a demon out of a man, and the people were wondering if He might be Israel's Messiah: "This man cannot be the Son of David, can he?" (v. 23). When the Pharisees heard this, they wanted to silence any such talk because they hated Jesus. So, they accused Jesus of casting out demons by the power of Satan. Jesus replied, "Any kingdom divided against itself is laid waste; and any city or house divided against itself will not stand. If Satan casts out Satan, he is divided against himself; how then will his kingdom stand?" (vv. 25–26). We should never expect Satan to go against himself.

Jesus went on to apply this to Himself in Matthew 12:28–29 when He said that He cast out demons by the Spirit of God. Then He used this illustration: "How can anyone enter the strong man's house and carry off his property, unless he first binds the strong man? And then he will plunder his house."

Jesus was saying that He was able to plunder Satan's house because He is stronger than Satan. And the reason He can overcome whatever Satan is trying to do in your life is that what He is doing is greater than what Satan is trying to do. So when it comes to the angelic realm, there is complete loyalty. Satan will never betray himself. God will never betray His kingdom. It's only *people* who want to vacillate between the two kingdoms. Angels don't vacillate. Angels don't sit on the spiritual fence. You don't see angels with one foot in the world and one foot in heaven. Angels are full-time with God or full-time with Satan.

This principle of loyalty is important for our lives and our spiritual warfare. How much of the power of God you see in your life depends on whether you are a full-time or a part-time saint. If you're a part-time saint, then don't expect to see the full-time presence of God in your life, because friendship with the world is hostility toward God (James 4:4). The only way you're going to see God's authority operating in your life is if your total allegiance is to Him and His kingdom. God has called us to be full-time disciples, and it is in His realm that He transfers His authority to us (Matt. 28:18–20).

Exercising Authority

One of the primary ways angels carry out their ministry in history is through people. Again, this principle applies to both good and evil angels. Paul warns, "The Spirit explicitly says that in later times some will fall away from the faith, paying attention to deceitful spirits and doctrines of demons" (1 Tim. 4:1). This verse clearly says that some of the teaching that will come in the last days is demonic in origin. But how does this teaching come? Through liars (v. 2), men who try to get God's people to abstain from that which He has provided.

In other words, the demons are promoting Satan's agenda through people they control. These may even be people who don't know they are being controlled by demons. But they are teaching demonic doctrines and leading people astray from the truth. This is why it's so important that you not only stay in tune spiritually yourself, but stay around people who are spiritually in tune. One of the gifts of the Holy Spirit is the gift of discernment. We need discernment to tell if a problem or situation is being promoted by demons. If it is, then the solution needs to be spiritual, not just human.

This is why the Bible tells us to "test the spirits" (1 John 4:1). The first and most important test is found in verses 2–3. Every spirit that confesses Christ is from God, and every spirit that does not confess Christ is not from God. This test alone will help you sort out a lot of false teaching. We need to discern what is influencing people to do what they do and say what they say. This is also important because even though we as believers cannot be demon-possessed, we can be demon-influenced. We can allow Satan's way of thinking and acting to influence us.

I want to return to Daniel 10, this time to look at the matter of angels exercising their authority through human beings. Daniel had been praying and fasting for understanding from God for three weeks when an angel appeared to him (v. 5). And this angel was not a cute, chubby little Valentine cherub. Read Daniel 10:6–9, and you'll see that Daniel fell on his face, and the men with him ran away when he saw the angel. This was an awesome creature. The angel had to reassure Daniel and stand the prophet up so he could deliver his message. Then look at what the angel told Daniel:

> From the first day that you set your heart on understanding this and on humbling yourself before your God, your words were heard, and I have come in response to your words. But the prince of the kingdom of Persia was withstanding me for twenty-one days. (vv. 12–13a)

Here is a battle in heaven between an angel and a demon called "the prince of Persia." The demon had this title because he was exercising his power through people in the earthly kingdom of Persia, influencing this kingdom to oppose God's plan through Daniel and Israel. Notice that the battle had begun the moment Daniel started praying three weeks earlier. The demon was able to delay the good angel in delivering God's answer to Daniel.

Before we go any further, let me draw some crucial implications from this passage. First, Daniel 10 shows us that whether we receive an answer to our prayers often has everything to do with a battle we cannot see, because Satan wants to stop God's answer from getting through. You might be thinking, *Then why doesn't God just wipe out all the demons and His human enemies and clear the way? Get rid of them all, and then we wouldn't have to worry about it.* God could do that, of course, but He has chosen to win the spiritual battle by using different weapons. He wants to demonstrate that when His people are living in obedience to Him, they are greater than Satan and his hordes of demons who are operating in rebellion against Him. So if you're praying and the answer hasn't come yet, you need to start praying, "Lord, if You are using Your angel to send the answer to my prayer, I pray that You will provide him with whatever support he needs along the way to defeat whatever tries to delay or stop him."

Daniel didn't quit praying because his answer hadn't come at a certain time. If you don't know that this kind of unseen activity is going on, you may think that God either doesn't care or that He is mad at you. If you don't realize that the angelic world is seeking to exercise authority through people on earth, you will react unbiblically rather than persevering in prayer. As awesome as he was, the angel who appeared to Daniel had been unable to break through the demonic resistance. He couldn't get God's answer through to Daniel.

But then the angel invoked the principle of authority and sent for Michael to help him: "Then behold, Michael, one of the chief princes, came to help me, for I had been left there with the kings of Persia" (10:13b). Michael overruled the resistance of the demon of the kingdom of Persia and got the answer through to Daniel.

What God did for Daniel, He can do for you. So don't get discouraged or frustrated if your answer doesn't come right away or if it doesn't seem like God is working in your circumstance. Your answer is tied to events outside you, beyond you, and above you. And God may be using His angelic channels, so hold on until your answer comes.

My point is that behind nations and events, there is angelic activity. For example, later in the book of Daniel, Michael is called the angel "who stands guard over the sons of your people" (12:1). The reason Israel can't be destroyed is that Israel's wars are not only about human conflict. There is an archangel involved who says, "You will not be able to destroy this people."

ACTIVATED BY AUTHORITY

This brings me to a final point about the operation of angels: they are activated by authority. The passage that introduces us to this is 1 Corinthians 11, where Paul sets down this foundational principle of authority: "I want you to understand that Christ is the head of every man, and the man is the head of a woman, and God is the head of Christ" (v. 3). Then Paul goes into a discussion of praying and prophesying with and without head coverings. Whether this passage refers to a woman's long hair or to a covering over the hair is debated, but Paul's thesis is that the woman should have her head covered when engaging in these activities, as a sign of her submission to God-ordained authority. Then Paul makes this summary statement in verse 10: "Therefore the woman ought to have a symbol of authority on her head, because of the angels."

First Corinthians 11 has to do with the church's worship and how that worship is supposed to work. What I believe Paul is saying here is that in order for the angels to do what they're supposed to do, the people for whom they are doing it must do what they are supposed to do. Paul has argued that it is a disgrace and a sign of rebellion against authority for a woman to pray or speak in church with her head uncovered. If a woman did that and signaled her rebellion with the angels watching, she would rebuff the angels.

The woman is not the only person under authority here. Men are to operate under the authority of Christ. And Paul says that even Christ is subject to God the Father. Men and women are equal in essence but distinct in function. And when you rebel against that chain of command, you lose access to the angelic involvement and activity in your life.

I suspect that many women are not seeing the power of God operating in their lives, are not seeing their prayers answered, are not seeing God intervene in their circumstances, because they have decided to address things by means of rebellion rather than by means of biblically based obedience. The same thing can be said of men. When we rebel against the authority of Christ over our lives, we place ourselves outside God's protective angelic hedge, and the enemy has a field day with us. The angels are activated when God's people are operating according to His principles of authority. The holy angels are under God's sovereign authority.

That's good news for you and me because one reason why we are going to win this conflict called spiritual warfare is that the angels are under God's authority. In fact, the danger in a study like this is that as you begin to get plugged into these spiritual realities and begin to recognize angelic activity in your life, you will be tempted to worship angels. People in the Bible who saw angels often faced the temptation to worship them because they are such overwhelming creatures. For instance, when the apostle John saw the angel in Revelation 19, he said, "I fell at his feet to worship him. But he said to me, 'Do not do that; I am a fellow servant of yours . . .; worship God'" (v. 10). Again in 22:8, John fell at the feet of an angel to worship him, and the angel said, "Do not do that" (v. 9). No angel of God ever accepts worship. The angels know whose authority they are under and who is worthy of worship. Only one angel ever tried to steal God's worship, and his name was Lucifer. No angel has tried it since. The angels always direct all worship to God.

GOD DEMONSTRATING HIS AUTHORITY

In closing this chapter, let's look at a classic case that demonstrates the authority of God over the angels: the story of Job. God called the angels together for a conference in heaven, and He allowed Satan to attend the meeting (Job 1:6). You have to be pretty confident in your power to allow the enemy into your planning sessions. God not only allowed Satan to enter His presence, but also pointed out His servant Job to Satan: "Have you considered My servant Job? For there is no one like him on the earth, a blameless and upright man" (1:8). This was not a case of Satan looking for Job. According to verse 7, Satan was just roaming around on earth, looking for someone to devour like the roaring lion he is (see 1 Peter 5:8). God pointed out Job, and Satan replied, "Does Job fear God for nothing? Have You not made a hedge about him and his house and all that he has, on every side? You have blessed the work of his hands, and his possessions have increased in the land. But put forth Your hand now and touch all that he has; he will surely curse You to Your face" (Job 1:9–11).

Satan issued a challenge to God as part of the angelic conflict. Satan wanted to embarrass God by proving to Him that Job was not the man God thought he was. So God gave Satan permission to take everything Job had, except his life or his health (1:12). Here was Job, minding his business, going to work every day. And suddenly everything he had was gone, including his children. But Satan could not cross the line God had drawn because God was firmly in control, and Satan was under His authority.

Even later, when Satan again challenged God and was allowed to afflict Job with a terrible disease, God demonstrated His absolute control over the angelic realm by again drawing a line that Satan could not cross (Job 2:6). There is a whole chapter's worth of principles for our spiritual warfare in the life of Job. His faithfulness to God is incredible, despite the fact that he didn't know what was happening or why—and God never really told him. Job didn't understand all the ramifications of his circumstances, but he understood that he was part of something bigger, and he demonstrated his submission to God's authority.

Angels clearly only operate by authority. They function along lines of authority that are distinctly marked out by God, and the extent to which we will see the operation of angels in our lives is the extent to which we bring ourselves under God's authority as a way of life, like Job did. When we do that, then we can call on that authority for help in our time of need.

7

Enlisting Our Spiritual Allies

As we dive deeper into the study of the spiritual realm, I want to talk about enlisting the help of angels, or how you can best position yourself so that God can release His angels to minister on your behalf. We know from Hebrews 1:14 that angels are ministering spirits assigned to those who will inherit salvation. That is, angels have been given responsibility to serve those who know Jesus Christ. To be clear, I'm not suggesting that you and I can force the angelic world to do anything we want. The angels obey their boss, Jesus Christ. We have no authority in the angelic realm on our own. Our authority comes from our relationship with God through Christ.

Although we have authority by virtue of our position, not our obedience, we cannot expect guidance or answers to prayer unless we are obedient to God. But when we are in right relationship with God, He is predisposed to release angelic activity on our behalf as we carry out His purposes.

It's a matter of putting ourselves in a position for God to minister to us through the ministry of angels.

The means by which we enlist the angels to minister on our behalf is no great mystery or secret. The holy angels of God are active in their assistance of us when we worship Him. Hebrews says that when we come to worship God, we join the company of "myriads of angels" (12:22). The theology here is very straightforward. Angels were created for the worship of God. In fact, they are always looking into the face of God (Matt. 18:10). And when we join them in doing what they do best, God activates them on our behalf.

So in this chapter, I want to help you understand the implications of this statement as we look at the various categories of worship and learn what it takes to see the activity of the angels in our lives.

THE IMPORTANCE OF WORSHIP

I want to begin with a great passage, Isaiah 6. In this text, the angels and worship come together in a powerful way. We know from verse 1 that the prophet had his great vision "in the year of King Uzziah's death." That historical note may not mean much to you, but it meant a lot to Isaiah because under King Uzziah, Israel had finally flourished. It had come into its own. It had become a power to be reckoned with. And yet, Uzziah had died. It could be that as you read this, your Uzziah has died—something in your life that you were counting on to keep things steady has disappeared. It could be your job, your health, or some other circumstance. But whatever it was, it's gone. The hope you were placing in that thing, person, or set of circumstances is no longer available to you.

Isaiah's vision came at just the right time, because he and his nation were hurting. But he did the right thing by bowing before the Lord. It was in recognizing His proper relationship before God that Isaiah joined the angels, and the angels moved on God's behalf in his life:

> In the year of King Uzziah's death I saw the Lord sitting on a throne, lofty and exalted, with the train of His robe filling the temple. Seraphim stood above Him, each having six wings; with two he covered his face, and with two he covered his feet, and with two he flew. And one called out to another and said, "Holy, Holy, Holy, is the LORD of hosts, the whole earth is full of His glory."
> (vv. 1–3)

When Isaiah went into the temple in Jerusalem, he was suddenly transported to the temple in heaven, the realm that the New Testament calls heavenly places. And what did he see? He saw angels, the seraphim, doing in heaven what Isaiah came to the temple to do on earth—worship.

Whenever you and I worship God, we join the angels, because for them, worship is nonstop activity. The Bible says the seraphim had six wings. With two wings they covered their faces, because they could not look directly on the awesome glory of God. With two other wings they covered their feet, symbolizing humility in God's presence. And with two wings they flew, ready to do God's bidding. Please notice that four of the seraphim's wings are for worship, and two are for working. If you spend more time in worship than in working, then you'll know what you're doing when you go to work because you have been in God's presence.

ANGELS ARE
ENLISTED THROUGH PRAISE

These opening verses in Isaiah give us the setting of the vision and reveal the first area of worship in which the angels are involved. One fundamental element of worship is praise. In the midst of his worship, Isaiah heard the seraphim calling out their praise to God. They spoke antiphonally, calling out to one another, perhaps from each side of the temple. One group spoke, and the other answered in response.

Isaiah saw the Lord seated on a throne, "lofty and exalted." We call this attribute of God His transcendence, the fact that He is infinitely far above and distinct from everything in the universe. But the angels also sang, "The whole earth is full of His glory" (v. 3). This is the immanence of God, His nearness to His creation. Both are true of Him. He is "out there" and yet also right here.

Pay careful attention to the text. Isaiah went to the temple to worship God because King Uzziah had died. Isaiah's earthly circumstances were a mess. But when he went into the temple, he learned something he couldn't learn by Googling it. The internet headlines said, "The King Is Dead." But the temple headlines said, "The King Is Alive." Do you see the difference? Which news source are you going to read? Which headline are you going to focus on? If you look at your circumstances through earthly eyes only, they may look bad. But when you come into the temple of God and learn what God is about, it changes the way you view your circumstances.

Isaiah saw God.

When you come into the house of God to worship, things can change. Maybe on Saturday your King Uzziah died. Your world took a tumble. But then you saw God on Sunday, and there was new hope. There was a new sense that all was not lost. That's what God does when you worship.

When Isaiah saw and heard the angels worshiping, something happened: "The foundations of the thresholds trembled at the voice of him who called out, while the temple was filling with smoke" (v. 4). This wasn't a tame worship service! Isaiah—an incredibly spiritual man—saw all of this and cried out, "Woe is me, for I am ruined!" (v. 5). He was basically saying, "I thought I was good until I came in here. I sing my songs, but I don't sing so that the building shakes. I believe in God, but I've never seen Him like this."

Isaiah got to see God as He really is. As a result, the prophet saw himself as he really was. He saw how unlike God he was. When you get a new view of God in His holiness, you get a new view of yourself. And it's not pretty.

The word *woe* means "undone," literally "coming apart at the seams." Isaiah saw his sin and the sin of his people, and he confessed, "I am a man of unclean lips, and I live among a people of unclean lips; for my eyes have seen the King, the

Lord of hosts" (v. 5). It was at this point that the angels got active. After Isaiah allowed God—not the death of King Uzziah—to define his circumstances, the angels started to move. Verses 6–7 describe the prophet's cleansing by a seraph that flew to him with a burning coal from the altar.

Why did God send an angel to purify Isaiah? God had a mission for him: "Then I heard the voice of the Lord, saying, 'Whom shall I send, and who will go for Us?' Then I said, 'Here am I. Send me!'" (v. 8). Isaiah discovered what he was supposed to do with his life. Because he went into the temple to worship the Lord, he wound up joining the angels in bowing before God. And when God saw that, He sent the angels to prepare Isaiah for his mission.

You might be thinking, *But I'm confused. Praise God in your confusion. Why?* Because you are praising the One who can unconfuse your confusion.

There's another great example of the power of praise in 2 Chronicles 20. Jehoshaphat, the king of Judah, was in trouble. He was being invaded by three armies (v. 1). So Jehoshaphat prayed: "O Lord, the God of our fathers, are You not God in the heavens? And are You not ruler over all the kingdoms of the nations? Power and might are in Your hand so that no one can stand against You" (v. 6). That's not how most of us would start our prayer if three armies were invading us. We would start our prayer like this: "God, how could You let this happen to me?" But Jehoshaphat started praising God for who He is. Then he praised God for what He had done. "Did You not, O our God, drive out the inhabitants of this land before Your people Israel?" (v. 7). Then notice what Jehoshaphat said in verse 9: "Should evil come upon us, the sword, or judgment, or pestilence, or famine, we will stand before this house and before You . . . and cry to You in our distress."

Do you hear what he was saying? Jehoshaphat was saying, in effect, "Lord, whatever happens, we are going to worship You." And because he worshiped, he could say, "O our God, will You not judge them? For we are powerless before this great multitude who are coming against us; nor do we know what to do, but our eyes are on You" (v. 12).

Jehoshaphat and Judah not only worshiped, but prioritized worship over military strength. According to verse 21, the king commanded the praise singers to lead the army into battle. He knew that in order to win this fight, he needed God's help. If victory was to be gained, it would be gained by God's presence and power. No wonder we read in verse 22 that when the singers began singing and praising God, He ambushed and routed their enemies.

Today, we buy all kinds of stuff to solve our problems. We pay people to listen to us talk so we can solve our problems. We hire businesses to come up with solutions. But often God is saying, "If you would just praise, I would take care of that for you." Worship is what gets God's attention and enlists the help of His angels. And in 2 Chronicles 20, worship is what prompted God to come to the aid of His people and rout their enemies.

Friend, learn to praise God, and He will take care of the enemy.

ANGELS ARE
ENLISTED THROUGH PRAYER

A second element of worship that will enlist the angels on our behalf is prayer. When God's people pray, they move heaven. Prayer and the presence of angels are tied very closely together in Scripture. Many times, when God sent an angel to earth, it was in response to someone talking to the Lord. The experience of Peter in Acts 12 is a good example. Peter was in prison, and the church was praying. God sent an angel, and Peter was miraculously released. If you want to move the hand of God, pray like you expect something to happen.

God is sovereign and will make the ultimate decisions about our lives. But never let it be said in heaven that a lot of blessings were never delivered to you on earth because you either didn't pray or didn't expect anything to happen when you did pray. If you have a legitimate request or need, take it to God in prayer and expect an answer. Follow the example of Abraham. He interceded for Lot (Gen. 18), and two angels came to deliver Lot and his family from Sodom.

Another great example is found in Daniel 6, the great story of Daniel in the lions' den. Many of us need to review this account because we're being devoured by people and circumstances in our lives. A lot of people are in a lions' den today. Let's see what to do.

Daniel's problem started when his enemies persuaded the king to forbid prayer to any being but him for thirty days. They knew that Daniel would ignore the king's edict and pray to God. They were right (v. 10). Daniel was a praying man, but prayer did not keep him from getting thrown into the lions' den. People often think, *Because I pray, nothing bad should happen to me.* Not necessarily. Because you pray, you're not alone if something bad should happen. That's a big difference we need to understand.

Daniel wound up in the lions' den, but God honored His praying servant and sent an angel to shut the lions' mouths. Daniel was able to announce his own deliverance to the king the next morning (v. 22). The lions lost their appetite through angelic intervention. Daniel could have tried all he wanted to close the lions' mouths himself. A lot of us are doing everything we can to close the mouths of the things that are devouring us. But it doesn't work.

God's angels can do a better job with the lions in our lives than we can. But to get God's angels working on our lions, we have to get God's attention. And one way to get God's attention is through prayer.

Jesus understood the importance of prayer because He was a true man. In Luke 22:41, we find Jesus praying in the Garden of Gethsemane just before His crucifixion: "He withdrew from [the disciples] about a stone's throw, and He knelt down and began to pray, saying, 'Father, if You are willing, remove this cup from Me; yet not My will, but Yours be done.' Now an angel from heaven appeared to Him, strengthening Him" (Luke 22:41–43). Jesus was praying that He might be spared the cup of suffering that awaited Him at the cross. But then He submitted His will to the Father's will, and God the Father sent an angel to strengthen Jesus so He could accomplish the Father's will.

There's nothing wrong with praying for God to do certain things in your life. Jesus prayed fervently and specifically that God would remove the cross from His life. But then after He made His request, Jesus made it clear that what He wanted most was what God the Father wanted. Tell God what you want when you pray. That means you can't just pray, "Bless me today, Lord." That is a wasted prayer, because you haven't asked for anything. Vague prayers get vague answers. If you are still alive at the end of the day, you can assume that God blessed you that day. Don't be afraid to be specific in prayer. Tell God the desires of your heart. And when He gives you some of those desires, praise Him.

There is another kind of praise for answered prayer. This is not praise because we received what we asked for, but praise because even though God denied or delayed our request, He gave us the strength to accept what He sent us. When you pray, God will either give you what you asked for, or He will give you strength to deal with what He wants. Jesus was strengthened by an angel after He submitted to the Father's will and needed strength to go to the cross. So when you pray, "Thy will be done," God's strength will be yours. Prayer is a powerful way to enlist God's help, which may come through His angels.

ANGELS ARE
ENLISTED BY SUBMISSION

A third aspect of worship that can bring you angelic assistance is submission, which simply means coming underneath appropriate, God-appointed authority. Jesus in the Garden of Gethsemane was the perfect example of proper submission expressed in worship as He submitted to His Father's will. We have already made the point that angels themselves always operate under authority. You have the potential to significantly reduce the level of angelic help you receive from God if, for instance, you're a wife who is fighting the legitimate authority of your husband, or a husband who refuses to bow to Christ's authority over you. Angels know when we're operating in proper submission.

In Acts 19, we read about an unusual incident when a group of Jewish exorcists tried to imitate Paul's power over demons:

> Some of the Jewish exorcists, who went from place to place, attempted to name over those who had the evil spirits the name of the Lord Jesus, saying, "I adjure you by Jesus whom Paul preaches." Seven sons of one Sceva, a Jewish chief priest, were doing this. And the evil spirit answered and said to them, "I recognize Jesus, and I know about Paul, but who are you?" And the man, in whom was the evil spirit, leaped on them and subdued all of them and overpowered them, so that they fled out of that house naked and wounded. (vv. 13–16)

The angelic realm knows whether a person is functioning under authority. The demon knew that these men had no authority to be doing what they were doing. They had no right to be using the name of Jesus the way Paul used it. So, the demon knew that they were totally unprotected, and he messed them up.

If you're not under authority, your own authority is limited. God does not trust full use of His authority to people who have not first learned submission. Even Jesus "learned obedience from the things which He suffered" (Heb. 5:8). The apostle James makes this crucial connection when he writes, "Submit therefore to God. Resist the devil and he will flee from you" (James 4:7). Most people start quoting this verse by saying, "Resist the devil." But the first step is to submit to God. Come under His authority. Why? Until you've submitted to God, you won't have the power to resist the devil. But when you're submitted to God, the devil can't handle you because you are operating under God's authority, not his.

Nathanael got to see the angels in action because he recognized Jesus for who He is and came under Jesus' authority by responding to His call to discipleship (John 1:46–51). Isn't that what you want to see in your life, the angels of God bringing answers from heaven to your needs on earth? It won't happen until you come under the authority of Christ and exercise the responsibility you have under His authority. When you get all of that lined up properly, you will experience the ministry of angels, who address needs on earth with the resources of heaven.

ANGELS ARE ENLISTED BY WITNESS

Our discussion is incomplete, however, unless we address the issue of witness. In Luke 12:8–9, Jesus says, "Everyone who confesses Me before men, the Son of Man will confess him also before the angels of God; but he who denies Me before men will be denied before the angels of God." Jesus says your witness, or lack thereof, is an issue that involves the angels. This is because the angels are messengers who wait for God's instructions to bring the answers to earth. So if you're a Christian who can never seem to speak a word for Christ, then He will deny you angelic assistance when you come with your needs and requests. But if you are not ashamed to be publicly identified with Christ, if you don't mind other people knowing that you belong to Him, He will not be ashamed to say before the angels, "She is one of Mine. Take her the answer."

I want to close this chapter with four powerful verses from Psalm 103:

> The LORD has established His throne in the heavens,
>   And His sovereignty rules over all.
> Bless the LORD, you His angels,
> Mighty in strength, who perform His word,
> Obeying the voice of His word!
> Bless the LORD, all you His hosts,
> You who serve Him, doing His will.
> Bless the LORD, all you works of His,
> In all places of His dominion;
> Bless the LORD, O my soul! (vv. 19–22)

This is an awesome picture of worship. Angels worship the Lord. His people worship Him. Even His works worship

Him. What about you? Worship is powerful, and God is looking for worshipers (John 4:23). When you worship, you exalt the Lord. And when He is exalted, when He is lifted up, He sends the angels on your behalf, to provide the answers and resources you need in the thick of the battle.

8

The Source
of Your Authority

Now that we have reviewed the angelic world, both the holy and the evil angels, and have come to understand something of what they are like and what they do, we are ready to move on. With this chapter we begin a new section of our study. We have learned that this world is Satan's domain. For now, he is "the ruler of this world" (John 12:31). And because Adam turned the world over to the evil one, Satan exercises a certain amount of authority.

But God in His grace thwarted Satan's attempt to take over completely. God's plan would be fulfilled even in Adam's failure because God promised that one day His seed would come through the woman to crush Satan (Gen. 3:15). In the meantime, however, we are caught in the middle of this battle. And because we are engaged in this angelic conflict, what we need is the power, the authority, to wage victorious warfare. We need to keep Satan from destroying our families, breaking up our marriages, owning our children, influencing our minds, and inflaming our passions. We need to get the devil off our backs.

But where does the authority for successful spiritual warfare come from? We are introduced to the source in Hebrews 2, where we discover that the answer is a person. The author of Hebrews says that God has another person in the spiritual battle, and he tells us that we need to *see* this person: "We do see Him who was made for a little while lower than the angels, namely, Jesus, because of the suffering of death crowned with glory and honor, so that by the grace of God He might taste death for everyone" (v. 9).

If we are going to be warriors in spiritual battle day in and day out, week after week, we need to see Jesus. The key to having authority in spiritual warfare is to "see Jesus"—to understand and put into practice all that He has purchased for us by His death, resurrection, and ascension. If we could only see Jesus, we would see Someone who has already won the battle for us. When we don't see Jesus, we don't have authority in the realm of the angelic conflict and spiritual warfare. When we can see Jesus in the sense I just described, we will receive authority we never knew possible.

Therefore, I want us to see and understand three important things about Jesus and His purchase of authority for us: the person of Jesus, the payment of Jesus, and your position in Jesus.

THE PERSON OF JESUS

When Adam sinned, God's promise of a seed from the woman who would crush the serpent's head was also a warning to Satan that the battle was not over. It appeared that Satan had won a big round, but someday a descendant of Eve would give birth to a baby who would crush Satan. Why did God decide that the ultimate victory over the devil would come through the human line? God could have crushed Satan at any moment in a blast of sovereign power. But God wanted to demonstrate His power over Satan through another plan, using the weakness and frailty of human flesh to defeat the powerful ruler of the evil spirit world.

The promise of Genesis 3:15 was made in the ancient past. But God made good on it one night in a stable in Bethlehem. Paul put it this way: "When the fullness of the time came, God sent forth His Son, born of a woman, born under the Law" (Gal. 4:4). Between the time of God's promise and its fulfillment in Jesus Christ, God had put in place the sacrificial system of the Mosaic Law to cover sin until the Savior would come. The Law provided temporary relief for sin until it was time for the Savior. The Israelites brought bulls and goats to offer on the altar to cover their sin. And every time an animal was sacrificed, it was a way of affirming, "One day a woman is going to have a baby who is going to crush Satan's head."

When it was just the right time, when all the conditions God wanted were in place, Jesus was born of a woman. Jesus was born while the Law was still in effect. He lived under the Law, but He came to make the final payment for sin and thus fulfill the Law. Don't read Galatians 4:4 too quickly, or you will miss something incredibly significant about Jesus. The One who purchased our authority over the devil is not just another spiritual warrior. He is God in the flesh. The Scripture is precise here. Paul said the Son was "sent," but the baby was "born." The Son existed before the baby was born. Isaiah said the same thing: "A child will be born to us, a son will be given to us" (Isa. 9:6). The child had to come through the birth canal, but the Son already existed.

In the person of Jesus, we have what theologians call the "hypostatic union" of deity and humanity, the two natures of Christ. The Son, the second person of the Holy Trinity, became human. He was the seed of the woman. The baby forming in Mary's womb was God in the flesh.

God had to have a man to fulfill the promise of Genesis 3:15—but this Man had to be the kind of man who would not do what Adam did. He had to be the kind of Man who could face the devil one-on-one and never yield. What God needed was the God-man, Jesus Christ. So God sent His Son, born of a woman, to reclaim the dominion that Adam had handed over to Satan.

Satan knew he was in trouble when the time came for Jesus to be born. So the enemy pulled out all the stops in his warfare against the Savior. Satan tried to foul things up before Jesus was born by subjecting Mary to humiliation and causing Joseph to consider divorcing her. But the fullness of God's time had come, and Jesus was born. Then the devil turned to King Herod for help, stirring him up to kill the babies in and around Bethlehem. Satan was doing everything he could because he had a big problem on his hands.

Remember, Satan does not possess all knowledge. He is not God's equal. In the birth of Jesus, God threw Satan the proverbial curveball. The devil had been rolling along, defeating person after person because he knew there was no man who could handle him. But Satan didn't count on God becoming a man. That was part of the plan he didn't calculate. He had been saying to God, "Give me another Adam. I can take care of him. Give me 'Adam Jr.' No problem. Just keep those Adams coming, because there is not a man You can create who can stand against my angelic power. Who do You have to handle me?" God said, "Try this one. I am going to send My Son to earth to become a Man and defeat you."

So the eternal God entered time and space as a Man. Satan tried to destroy Jesus, but none of his ideas worked. Please notice, by the way, that God used the angels to thwart Satan at every turn. The birth account of Jesus is filled with angelic visitations. It was an angel who announced the birth of Christ to shepherds. It was an angel who led Joseph and Mary to take their baby to Egypt, out of Herod's reach (Matt. 2:13).

When killing Jesus didn't work, Satan tried to overthrow Him by the temptation in the wilderness. The devil tried to get Jesus to do the same thing Adam did—act independently of God. And at one point, Satan used the same tactic: food. Satan must be big on food. Satan told Adam and Eve, "Eat this fruit." He told Jesus, "Why don't You turn these stones into bread?" (see Matt. 4:3). Adam ate apart from God's will and failed. Jesus refused to eat outside of God's will and won the battle.

Why did Jesus have to go to all the trouble and suffering of fasting for forty days in the wilderness and then face Satan head-on in intense spiritual combat? Why didn't Jesus just exercise His deity and destroy Satan right there in the wilderness? For the same reason God didn't crush Satan the moment he rebelled or in the Garden of Eden. He had a different plan, one that would display His power and grace. Jesus had to win the battle as a Man, as the seed of the woman. In fact, Jesus lived His whole life on earth with the limitations of humanity. Don't get me wrong. Jesus was fully God in flesh, but He voluntarily submitted to the limits of humanity. Even when Jesus performed a miracle, He did it in dependence upon His Father.

Jesus lived as a Man to demonstrate that He had the right to rule and to challenge Satan based on His obedience and dependence upon God. So Jesus fasted in the wilderness for spiritual power and then pulled out God's Word and shut Satan down.

If only the first Adam had used the Word of God when Satan tempted him and his wife. If only Adam had reminded Eve, "God said we can't eat from this tree." Adam didn't use the Word, but Jesus did—and He emerged victorious.

Satan wasn't finished, though. He had one more strategy to defeat Jesus—the cross. So according to Luke 22:3, Satan entered into Judas Iscariot, motivating him to betray Jesus Christ into the hands of His crucifiers. Things looked bad for Jesus at the cross. But the cross did not catch God by surprise. He already had a plan in place that would turn what Satan thought was his finest moment into his worst defeat! Jesus came "to destroy the works of the devil" (1 John 3:8). God would use the cross, an instrument of death and destruction, to destroy Satan's power and purchase for us all the authority we would ever need for spiritual victory.

THE PAYMENT OF JESUS

In order to conquer Satan, Jesus had to conquer death, because death is Satan's weapon. But to conquer death, Jesus had to pay for sin, since death is the consequence of sin. It was sin that brought death into the world, because God has decreed, "The soul who sins will die" (Ezek. 18:4). There's only one way to pay for sin, and that's through death. And there's only one way to conquer death, and that's through resurrection. You need resurrection power to conquer death. Somebody has to get up from the dead if death is going to be defeated.

This is what Jesus did in His payment for sin. He entered the realm of death, which is Satan's domain, and beat the devil in his own territory. Death is the last enemy (1 Cor. 15:26), one that none of us has ever been able to beat. So anyone who can beat death has broken the power of the biggest weapon Satan has.

Paul describes our problem and the payment Jesus made for sin in this classic passage:

When you were dead in your transgressions and the un-
circumcision of your flesh, He made you alive together
with Him, having forgiven us all our transgressions,
having canceled out the certificate of debt consisting
of decrees against us, which was hostile to us; and He
has taken it out of the way, having nailed it to the cross.
(Col. 2:13–14)

We were dead in sin and without hope, because we had
a "certificate of decrees" posted against us. This is a significant phrase. In Roman law, when a person was convicted of
a crime and imprisoned, a list of his offenses was drawn up
and posted on his cell door. This was his certificate of decrees, showing why he was in prison. Anybody who walked
by his cell could see why a person was in prison because of
the certificate of decrees.

Jesus Christ had a certificate like this posted over His
cross. Remember that after Pilate had tried Jesus, he went
out to the crowd and said, "I find no guilt in this man" (Luke
23:4). But the people shouted, "If you release this Man,
you are no friend of Caesar" (John 19:12), because Jesus
had claimed to be King of the Jews. Pilate yielded and con-
demned Jesus, but in order to crucify the Lord, he needed
a certificate of decrees to show why this Man was being executed. So, Pilate had a sign posted at the top of Jesus' cross,
written in Hebrew, Greek, and Latin: "Jesus of Nazareth,
King of the Jews."

As far as the crowd was concerned, Jesus was being cru-
cified for treason against Rome. The Jewish nation wanted

Him executed for blasphemy because He called Himself God. And as far as Satan was concerned, he was eliminating the seed of the woman who was going to crush him. But little did Satan know that there was another certificate of decrees posted above Jesus' cross. This was a divine certificate, drawn up by God, bearing the name of Tony Evans and every other person who has ever lived or who will ever live. This certificate contained every sin of every person, and every charge on that certificate was valid. We were hopelessly guilty—and the sentence for those sins was death.

But Jesus bore the punishment for all the sins of those who put their faith and trust in Him. He took our guilt. The Bible says that Jesus Christ did not die as innocent, but as guilty: "[God] made Him who knew no sin to be sin on our behalf, so that we might become the righteousness of God in Him" (2 Cor. 5:21).

Now we get to the good part. When a criminal had finished his sentence and paid his debt to society, his certificate of decrees was taken off his cell door and stamped with one Greek word: *tetelestai*, "paid in full." The certificate was canceled and handed to the former criminal, so he could prove to anyone who asked that he was now free. Those charges could never be brought against him again.

What were Jesus' last words on the cross? "It is finished!" (John 19:30). This was actually just one word: "*Tetelestai!*" The debt that you and I owed to God was paid by Jesus Christ, completely.

Why were the charges against us "hostile to us" (Col. 2:14)? For one, they carried the death penalty, but also because Satan could always bring them up against us. Satan knows that God in His holiness cannot tolerate sin, so Satan delights in bringing up the charges against us. He loves to accuse people. He tells God, "Look at what this person has done. I have the certificate right here. Look at the charges against him."

But when Satan goes before God and brings up Tony Evans, Jesus Christ steps in and says, "Look at the stamp on his certificate. His debt has been paid in full. I have paid for sins he has not even committed yet." That's why once you are saved, you can never be lost again. Jesus paid the full price for your sins before you were even born. He satisfied the demands of God against sin.

Jesus' death took care of the sin problem. God's wrath against sin has been satisfied, and He is now free to declare us forgiven because the debt has been paid. But there was still an authority problem. Jesus had to deal with the question of who rules the universe. That brings us to what happened between the time of Jesus' death and His resurrection. This is "the rest of the story."

Jesus not only purchased the forgiveness for our sins by His death, but also reclaimed the authority of the universe that Adam had relinquished by his sin (see Matt. 28:18). Satan and his demons in the underworld needed to hear the announcement of Jesus' victory. So did the saints who had died before Calvary and were in a place called "paradise" or Abraham's bosom (see Luke 16:23). So while Jesus' body was lying in the tomb, Jesus in His spirit went to Hades.

In the Bible, Hades is not the same as the lake of fire, or

eternal hell. Hades was the temporary abode of those who died before the coming of Christ. Everyone who died before Calvary went to Hades, because Hades had two compartments in it. Jesus' story of the rich man and Lazarus in Luke 16 is the clearest picture we have of this temporary arrangement. Lazarus died and went to paradise, but the rich man died and woke up in torment (v. 23). The two could see each other, but they were separated by "a great chasm" (v. 26).

Why didn't Lazarus go to heaven as we know it, and the rich man to the eternal lake of fire? Because God was still operating on the "layaway" plan—the Old Testament system that provided only a temporary holding place. It wasn't until the death of Christ that the final matters relating to eternal destiny were settled.

But Jesus made the final payment on the layaway plan. What happens when you make the last payment on a layaway? You get to take the merchandise home with you. That's exactly what Jesus did, according to Ephesians 4:8: "When He ascended on high, He led captive a host of captives." Jesus went in spirit to the paradise compartment of Hades and announced to those Old Testament saints, "I have paid the price. It's time to go home." Then He led those saints in a great march to heaven in the greatest "shuttle service" in history. This is why Jesus could tell the thief on the cross, "Today you shall be with Me in Paradise" (Luke 23:43). Jesus also visited the torment side of Hades, where He announced His victory to the lost souls in Hades and the devil and his crew (1 Peter 3:18–20). Jesus' proclamation was, "Satan, I declare total victory over you."

Satan didn't anticipate that Christ's death would satisfy God's justice in such a way that God could show His love to sinners without compromising His holiness. You may say, "But how do we really know God did all this?" When you pay the price for something, you get a receipt to show that the purchase was made and the full price was paid. You don't want any doubt. You don't want anyone to think that you didn't really pay for the merchandise. Your receipt is your proof. God gave us a receipt to prove that Jesus paid the price for sin, and to show that His payment was accepted.

The resurrection was proof that God was satisfied with Jesus' death and payment for sin. Several times in the book of Acts, the apostles appealed to the fact that God raised Jesus from the dead to prove that He was the Christ. Peter said there were many witnesses who saw the resurrected Christ (Acts 2:32).

So what did Jesus' victory do to Satan? Go back to Colossians 2:15, where Paul writes, "When He had disarmed the rulers and authorities, He made a public display of them, having triumphed over them through Him [Christ]." When Jesus rose from the dead, Satan was disarmed. He was stripped of his weapons (the literal meaning of "disarmed"). He lost all of his ammunition, and he was rendered powerless (Heb. 2:14). Jesus Christ went into Satan's territory of death and took away the captives of death who were waiting in paradise. Then Jesus beat death by rising from the dead. And He took away the fear and pain of death for all those who believe in Him.

Satan's best weapon was deactivated. The roaring lion

(1 Peter 5:8) had his teeth pulled out. The devouring lion was overcome by the Lion of the tribe of Judah, and now Satan is on a leash. We now have authority over Satan, not in and of ourselves, but because we belong to Christ.

OUR POSITION IN CHRIST

So we understand the person of Christ, that He had to be a Man empowered by God to defeat Satan. We understand the payment of Christ, that He died to pay for sin and to triumph over the devil. But if we are going to be victorious in our conflict with Satan, we also need to understand our position in Christ.

Because we don't know who we are in Christ, we don't know how to relate to our enemy the devil. We have powerful Christians living powerless lives because they keep looking to Satan for permission to live as Christians. But Satan is only powerful in our lives when we allow him to be powerful. This is why Jesus' triumph did not end with the resurrection. Jesus told His disciples He had to leave them. He was ascending back to heaven as a High Priest to take His blood and apply it to the mercy seat in heaven. And He was ascending as a triumphant King to be enthroned at the Father's right hand, from where He rules all of creation today. "All authority has been given to Me in heaven and on earth" (Matt. 28:18).

Jesus Christ was enthroned by God the Father, and all powers came under His authority, including the power of Satan and his demons. Earlier in Colossians 2, Paul had written, "In [Christ] all the fullness of Deity dwells in bodily form, and in Him you have been made complete, and He is the head over all rule and authority" (vv. 9–10). According to Ephesians 1:20–22, when God raised Christ from the dead, He "seated Him at His right hand in the heavenly places, far above all rule and authority and power and dominion. . . . And He put all things in subjection under His feet."

Jesus Christ rules over all from His throne in the heavenlies, and he has "render[ed] powerless him who had the power of death, that is, the devil" (Heb. 2:14). Moreover, we have been raised up with Christ and are seated with Him "in the heavenly places" (Eph. 2:6). Jesus Christ not only sits enthroned, but we sit enthroned with Him. He has partnered with us to share His victory with us.

The word *triumphed* in Colossians 2:15 pictures the parade given to a victorious Roman general, who would bring his spoils and his captives in chains back to Rome and put them on display. Jesus triumphed so completely over Satan that He is marching the devil around in chains, displaying him as a whipped foe. And because we are in Christ, we share in His victory.

Jesus Christ triumphed over the devil through His blood. It was the blood of Jesus that paid for our sin and secured for us a place of authority with Him in the heavenly places. That's why we see the saints overcoming the devil by the blood of the Lamb (Rev. 12:11).

Do you see why I say you must understand your position in Christ? You must know who you are in Christ and begin exercising your authority under His authority. You can't beat Satan in your own authority, because you don't have any. The key is that you have been raised and seated with Christ. Satan knows he can handle you, but he knows he can't handle Christ. The devil's strategy is to keep you from living your life in the power of Christ, claiming the authority that is yours because you are under His blood.

When a police officer directing traffic signals for you to stop, you stop. Why? Because that officer is wearing a uniform and a badge as symbols of authority. That officer standing in traffic doesn't have the power to make you stop. You can drive right on by. But because the officer is wearing the symbols of his or her authority, and because you know that officer has been delegated authority from the local police department to stop traffic, you honor that authority and obey the officer. The uniform says it all. But what happens if you don't honor the officer's authority and keep on driving? You will soon discover that the officer has real power to back up his or her authority because there will be cars with flashing lights coming after you to arrest you.

As a believer, you are clothed with Christ (Gal. 3:27). When Satan sees that uniform, he has to stop. Satan won't stop when he sees you trying to use the power of positive thinking. He won't stop because you are making New Year's resolutions to try to beat him. He's not impressed by your efforts, because he knows there's no authority behind them. He can run through your stop signal because he knows there is nobody there to back you up. But when you claim your authority through the blood of Christ, Satan has to stop.

Some of us believers are praying, "God, please give me

victory over the devil." God is saying in response, "You already have the victory. Put on your uniform." When you step out under the blood and the authority of Jesus Christ, when Satan comes after you, he has to pull up short.

FIGHTING FROM VICTORY

In your Christian life, you don't fight *for* victory; you fight *from* victory. You don't say, "I am going to try to be victorious over Satan today." Instead, you say, "Jesus Christ has already been victorious over Satan. So today, by faith, I am going to live in Christ's authority, trusting His blood to give me power over any attacks of the evil one." That's authority.

One day a butterfly was fluttering in great fright, because it was being pursued by a sparrow. The sparrow kept pecking at the butterfly, eager to devour it. But the butterfly was on the inside of a window, the glass separating it from the sparrow. The sparrow kept pecking, trying to get at the butterfly. And the butterfly kept fluttering around in terror at the presence of the sparrow. The butterfly couldn't understand that the pane of glass between him and the sparrow kept the sparrow from doing what it wanted to do. What scared the butterfly was that the sparrow was so close, right in his face. If only the butterfly could have understood that the pane of glass was all he needed for protection, no matter how close the sparrow seemed to be.

Tomorrow morning, Satan is going to be in your face again. He's going to be trying to devour you, to ruin your testimony and capture your marriage or virtue. But remember that Jesus Christ has slid a pane of glass in between you and Satan. This glass is red, stained with His blood. Satan can peck at you, and he may seem close. But he can't touch you without God's permission, because you are protected by the blood of Jesus Christ. You don't have to be afraid.

And one day, according to Revelation 20:1–3, you won't have to worry about Satan anymore. Because on that day, an angel from God will be sent down with a chain to wrap around Satan. And this one who deceived the nations will be thrown into the abyss for one thousand years. Jesus Christ will order an angel, perhaps Michael or Gabriel, to tie up Satan.

So when you get up tomorrow, get up in the authority of Jesus Christ. Overcome Satan by the blood of Christ, because He has purchased that authority for you. Live under Christ's authority, and you get Christ's authority. Then you can fight from a position of victory instead of fighting for victory. Jesus has already won the victory for you. Tell Him you want His authority, and then live in it by realigning your thoughts with His truth.

You live in Christ's authority when you choose to respond to life's challenges, fears, or temptations according to God's will and in His power. It's when you choose to face fear with the shield of faith, dismantle lies with the truth of God's Word, or regain focus by applying spiritual principles to your decisions and actions. Living in authority comes through surrender and transformation (see Rom. 12:1–2), allowing you to fight spiritual battles in a confidence rooted in what Jesus Christ has already secured for you. It is having a mindset based on your heavenly position (see Eph. 2:6). In that mindset, your emotions and responses align underneath and rest in God's rule and power rather than with Satan, his demons, and their influence on you.

One of the most strategic ways to live in the authority of Christ is by employing the spiritual weapons He has given us access to use. These weapons help you to fully carry out the full expression of Christ's authority in every aspect of your life. Let's look at these in the next chapter.

9

Our Weapons

Understanding the authority behind your victory is critical to living out the victory in warfare that Christ secured on the cross. And you must express that understanding to feel the full effect of the victory that is yours. We express our understanding of Christ's victory in warfare when we engage in the battle with the weapons that He has provided for us.

In the book of Ephesians, Paul doesn't waste any time in spelling out what these weapons are and how we are to use them for spiritual warfare. It's "the full armor of God" (6:11). The armor is something God gives us, not something we put together on our own. But before Paul gets to the armor, he gives us an important exhortation: "Be strong in the Lord and in the strength of His might" (v. 10).

This says the battle is the Lord's, not yours.

"Be strong in the Lord" is a passive command. That means God, not you, supplies the strength. Your job is to put on the armor He supplies, to be well-dressed for warfare.

That's exactly what Paul says in Romans 13:11–14. He tells us to wake up from our spiritual sleep and put on "the armor of light" (vv. 11–12).

What is armor of light? Paul explains it in verse 14 when he says, "Put on the Lord Jesus Christ." This is reality; this is spiritual war. We need to dress up in Jesus because the devil isn't one bit scared of you and me. The only person who has ever scared the devil is Jesus Christ.

Remember, you are not fighting people. The worst person in your life is not your problem. Satan is your problem, and he is using people and circumstances to get at you. So don't get sidetracked fighting people.

YOUR NEED FOR ARMOR

Let's talk about our need for the armor of God as Paul explains it in Ephesians 6. He writes, "Put on the full armor of God, so that you will be able to stand firm against the schemes of the devil" (v. 11). The key phrase here is "stand firm," which Paul repeats in verses 13 and 14.

The first reason you need God's armor is because of your enemy. Satan's attacks come from the unseen realm of the spirit. Therefore, if you don't use God's spiritual weapons to fight your spiritual battle, you are going to war with a water gun. For some of us, our water gun is our anger. We get mad and tell people off. But anger is a human weapon that doesn't work against a spiritual enemy.

Others of us have tried to use positive thinking or "positive confession," naming and claiming this and that. Or we make New Year's resolutions. But these water guns don't work in the war against Satan. You can't use human weapons to win a spiritual war. The devil is far too crafty for us. He has schemes and plans we can't even see. We need the armor of God because of the enemy we are up against.

The second reason you need God's armor is because of the nature of the victory Christ has won for us. Three times here in Ephesians 6, Paul tells us that our goal in spiritual warfare is to stand firm. That means to hold the ground Jesus has already won for us. One reason the church has so many defeated Christians on its hands is that they are still trying to whip Satan. That means they're fighting the wrong battle. We saw in Colossians 2:15 that Jesus has already beaten and embarrassed Satan. So all we have to do is stand firm.

We as believers are like a football team that's ahead 72–0 late in the game. When your team is up by that many points, winning is no longer the issue. You don't need to score any more points. You're only on the field to hold your ground and keep the other team from scoring. Satan is trying to rob you of spiritual victory and spiritual blessings you already possess. Ephesians 1:3 says God has already blessed us with every spiritual blessing it was possible to give us. Would you go out and borrow money if you already had a million dollars sitting in your bank account? Would you go out on the streets like a pauper and ask, "Buddy, can you spare a dime?" if your daddy owned it all? Some of us are walking around like spiritual paupers when Jesus Christ has credited to our account all of His power and authority. Our weapons are weapons of authority, because of the decisive victory Jesus has won for us.

A third reason you need your armor is found in an interesting phrase in Ephesians 6:13. Paul says we need to stand firm and resist Satan "in the evil day." The evil day is when your number comes up, so to speak. One translation puts it, "when things are at their worst" (NEB). You need the armor of God to stand firm when the evil day comes. In 1 Corinthians 16:13 Paul writes, "Stand firm in the faith." That's the key. You can stand firm because your faith is in the One who provides you with the armor. He has surrounded you with protection, so you don't have to worry about the enemy's attacks. God wants us to hold our ground and not budge when the evil day comes.

THE NAMES OF THE ARMOR

For the rest of the chapter, I want to look in detail at each piece of the armor God has provided for us. These are important weapons you must know how to wear and how to wield if you're going to make the most of the spiritual authority you have in Christ.

The Belt of Truth

The first piece of armor Paul names is the belt of truth. "Stand firm therefore, having girded your loins with truth" (Eph. 6:14a). The spiritual armor Paul describes in this chapter is patterned after the armor and weapons of a Roman soldier of the day. For instance, these soldiers wore a long tunic that flowed down to the ground. But when it came time to fight, the soldier picked up that tunic and tucked it in his belt so he would have mobility for battle.

A Roman soldier also carried his sword on his belt, and his breastplate connected to the belt too. So the belt was fundamental because everything else connected to it. Without his belt, a soldier couldn't keep himself together.

When you're up against a foe who's trying to rob your joy, your meaning, your future, your family, and even your life, you'd better not go out to battle without your belt of truth on. The belt of truth is becoming more and more important because we live in a world that no longer accepts objective truth. Everybody has an opinion, everybody has an idea. Truth today is totally relative, and "tolerance" is the current buzzword. That's why you'll hear people say, "What's true for you is not necessarily true for me." The devil will whip you if he finds you without your belt of truth.

We need to know God's truth because the devil is a liar. He thrives on lies, so if he can get you in an environment where there is no objective standard of truth, he will milk it for all it's worth.

Truth is the beginning point of authority. The belt of truth holds your life together and protects you from the lies of the evil one. The belt of truth also keeps us from replacing God's Word with our feelings.

If you want real weapons of spiritual authority, you have to be ready to say that when God's Word contradicts how you feel, then your feelings are wrong and God's Word is right.

Satan gets nervous when he sees that you are committed to God's truth because you haven't left him any loopholes he can get through. Satan is getting at a lot of believers because how they feel is more important to them than what God says.

The belt of truth goes around the "loins," the midsection. This is the area that provides strength to the body, but it is also a vulnerable area that needs protection. When your midsection is protected by truth, you are off to a good start, for Jesus Christ is truth (John 14:6).

The Breastplate of Righteousness

The second piece of armor is also found in Ephesians 6:14: "Stand firm therefore . . . having put on the breastplate of righteousness." The Roman soldier's breastplate protected his chest, his heart. The best protection for your heart in spiritual warfare is to be covered in Christ's righteousness. This is talking about our salvation. A lot of Christians don't understand all that happened to them when they got saved. A lot of Christians only know that Christ forgave their sins. But that's not all that happened. If you know Jesus Christ as your Savior, not only were your sins forgiven, but Christ gave you His perfect righteousness. That is, God credited the righteousness of Christ to your spiritual account. You are righteous today as a Christian because of this transfer.

The theological term for this transaction is imputation. Christ's righteousness was accredited to your account. As a Christian, you are not simply a forgiven sinner. You stand as righteous in God's sight as Jesus Himself, because Jesus' righteousness is wrapped around you like a robe. When

Satan accuses you, you can point to your righteous standing before God.

One reason so many Christians exercise so little authority in spiritual warfare is that they don't really know who they are. The breastplate of righteousness speaks of our exalted position in Christ. As we put it on each day, we are protected against Satan and his demons, because they can't hang out in an environment of righteousness. Of course, we fail at times and act unrighteously. But that's when we confess our sin (1 John 1:9) and keep on going. You don't lose your breastplate just because you blow it. Righteousness isn't just something you practice. It's your identity. You are righteous in Jesus Christ.

Because you are a righteous person, God is going to help you pursue things that enable you to act like who you are and help you avoid things that do not enhance your righteousness. This means He will have to discipline you on occasion, not because He doesn't want us to have any fun. No, He's after our long-term blessing. Your prayer each day as you put on the breastplate should be, "Lord, I thank You that You have already made me righteous. Help me today to live up to what I already am."

The Gospel of Peace

The third piece of spiritual armor we need to wear are the shoes of "the gospel of peace" (Eph. 6:15). If you are going to stand firm, you definitely need reliable footwear. Earlier in Ephesians, Paul had said that Jesus is our peace (2:14). So, we're still talking about getting dressed up in Jesus. The "gospel of peace," the good news of Jesus Christ, brings us not only truth and righteousness, but also peace of heart.

The Roman soldier wore shoes with cleats on them for surefootedness in battle. A soldier had to be able to stand and fight without slipping and sliding around because lost footing could be fatal.

Do you ever feel like your life is slipping and sliding all over the place? That's when you especially need to have the peace of God anchoring your feet and guarding your heart. We need to distinguish between the peace *of* God and peace *with* God. Peace with God comes only when you place your faith in Christ and become a Christian. Once you know Christ, you are in position to enjoy the peace of God, which He gives to His children each day as they prepare for spiritual warfare. But it's peace with God that is listed as the bit of equipment here. Paul says we need to be prepared with peace because the world we are going to face is not always peaceful. In fact, since we are engaged in a spiritual battle, we should expect turmoil.

But when we are wearing peace with God like shoes on our feet, we can handle whatever Satan brings against us—problems on the job, trouble with family—without stumbling. The peace of God can help you stand firm while Jesus deals with the enemy through you. When you get dressed each day, make sure you are wearing God's peace.

The Shield of Faith

The fourth piece of armor Paul tells us to take up is the shield of faith, which allows us to "extinguish all the flaming arrows of the evil one" (Eph. 6:16b). The shield that a Roman soldier carried into battle was about four and a half feet square. It was a huge shield that would even cover part of the body of the soldier fighting beside the shield holder. So Roman soldiers lined up side by side in close formation with their shields together, and all of them were covered as they advanced.

What is this shield of faith that is able to protect you from anything Satan could ever fire at you? It's acting on the truth that you say you believe. You take up the shield of faith when you take the truth that you "amened" on Sunday and live it out on Monday.

One of the best examples of what I'm talking about is Joshua at the battle of Jericho (Joshua 6). God told Joshua to have the Israelites march around the city once a day for six days, and then march around seven times on the seventh day. That must have seemed like a foolish thing to do. It didn't make sense militarily. It certainly wasn't accepted strategy for warfare. But God commanded Joshua to do it, and He promised to fight Israel's battle. So no matter how it looked to anyone else, Joshua took up the shield of faith and obeyed God. And God delivered Jericho into Joshua's lap.

I'm also reminded of Naaman, the Syrian commander who was covered with leprosy (2 Kings 5). Elisha told Naaman to go and dip seven times in the Jordan River to be cleansed. Naaman got insulted, because the Jordan is a dirty, muddy river. He didn't want to be embarrassed in front of his servants by having to dip in the Jordan. But his servants convinced him to do it, and Naaman did what God's prophet told him to do. He was healed because he chose to believe God.

Obeying God can sometimes seem foolish, difficult, or downright embarrassing. But God wants us to trust Him even when it doesn't make sense to trust Him. At times like these, we need to pick up our shield of faith and obey.

The Helmet of Salvation

The helmet of salvation (Eph. 6:17a) is the next piece of armor that can give you authority over the enemy. The helmet protects the head, the control center of the body. So the helmet of salvation covers a vital part. The purpose of a soldier's helmet was to absorb blows without causing damage to the head , much like a football player's helmet absorbs the shock of blows to his head.

Paul's reference to the helmet may imply our protection in a current spiritual battle, the way our salvation protects us from Satan's claim on our lives. Paul may also be thinking of the ultimate deliverance that salvation will bring, our hope for the future when our salvation is consummated. He uses the term *helmet* in this sense in 1 Thessalonians 5:8.

But in the context of spiritual warfare, we're talking about the battles you and I face every day. With the helmet of salvation protecting us, we have the authority we need to get on top of our circumstances instead of letting our circumstances bury us. When you ask people how they are, they will often reply, "Oh, I'm all right, under the circumstances." For the Christian, the response needs to be, "What are you doing under there?" When you pick up the helmet of salvation and put it on, you are saying to the devil that because of your salvation, God has given you victory over your circumstances. The helmet helps you fight from a position of victory.

We have let our circumstances rule us. And when circumstances rule us, we can't be in proper relation to God. So put on your helmet. Sure, Satan is trying to deliver a blow to your head. He knows where to strike. But the helmet of salvation can absorb the blow. The helmet allows you to say to Satan when he hits you with his best shot, "I can do all things through Him who strengthens me" (Phil. 4:13). The helmet reminds you that God "is able to keep you from stumbling" (Jude 24). The helmet's visor allows you to see Jesus and focus on Him. You won't get very far in spiritual warfare without your helmet.

The Sword of the Spirit

Now we're ready to complete the full armor of God. We do that when we take up "the sword of the Spirit, which is the word of God" (Eph. 6:17b). The sword mentioned here is not the soldier's long sword, but a short, dagger-like weapon about ten inches long. This sword had a needle-like point, and it was sharp on both sides. It was used for close-up fighting and could do some serious damage. It could cut an opponent coming and going. "The word of God is living and active and sharper than any two-edged sword," Hebrews 4:12 says.

What's interesting is that the term Paul uses for *Word* here does not refer to the Bible as a written book of truth, the way we normally think of the Word of God. This is not the Bible sitting on your coffee table or bookshelf. Instead, this is *rhema*, the utterance of God, the Word as it is spoken. Paul is talking about the use of the Word, not just its existence. Many of us go to church every Sunday with our Bible under our arm, but we don't always know how to wield it like a sword to slice the devil in half in spiritual battle.

The best example of wielding the Word was the temptation of Jesus. Satan attacked Jesus, but Jesus answered, "It is written," and then defeated Satan with the Word. Jesus didn't argue or dialogue with the devil. Jesus simply hit him with the Word, and the battle was over.

Satan loves to hear you and me talk to him and argue with him, because he knows our word doesn't have any authority from God to cut him in half. If we don't know the Word of God well enough to use it against the devil, no wonder we get defeated. No wonder we have no authority. The authority is in the Word.

That's the armor of God, the weapons of your authority. Is your armor in good shape? Are your belt, breastplate, and gospel shoes laid out when you go to bed, ready to be put on tomorrow? Are your shield, helmet, and sword close by, ready to be grabbed when needed? If so, then you're ready for the battle. And if you can't remember all the individual pieces of your spiritual armor, then just remember Christ. For if you have an intimate relationship with Him, you also have the armor.

THE WEAPON OF PRAYER

The weapons of your warfare won't do you a lot of good, though, if you don't know how to put them into action. We just spent some time looking at the six pieces of armor for spiritual warfare, but the apostle Paul doesn't stop writing there. In the very next verse, he gives us the secret to using this great authority God has made available. We might say that after describing the Christian's battle dress, Paul tells us how to get dressed, how to access the authority we possess: "With all prayer and petition pray at all times in the Spirit, and with this in view, be on the alert with all perseverance and petition for all the saints" (Eph. 6:18).

Prayer gains you access to the authority you need for victorious warfare.

Prayer is the way you get well-dressed for warfare.

The significance of prayer to spiritual warfare is evident in the very first word of Ephesians 6:18: "*With* all prayer" (italics added). With is a connecting word. Paul is saying that prayer is vitally connected to his discussion of spiritual warfare and the Christian's armor that has just preceded this verse.

Prayer is the atmosphere in which you are to fight. It's the way you stay in vital daily contact with your Commander. In other words, the way you activate the authority and use the armor described in Ephesians 6:10–17 is by prayer.

Remember, three times in this section (vv. 11, 13–14), Paul has told us to stand firm. That means to hold the territory Jesus Christ has won for us and not let the devil take any territory back. But the problem is that the devil has already taken back a lot of territory from many of us believers. He has taken back the territory of peace from some of us. From others, he has taken back the territory of our homes, our families, or our businesses. From others, the devil has taken back the authoritative position that God has given us. Satan is always looking to take back territory that Christ has won. So if we are going to stand firm, we must know how to put our armor on and how to use it. And that authority is activated through prayer.

The kind of prayer Paul has in mind here is intense, fervent, knowledgeable prayer that enables you to reach into heaven and make withdrawals from your spiritual account. Our job in the Christian life is not to add to what Christ has done. He has made all the deposits necessary for every spiritual need we will ever have. When God says we need to pray, He is inviting us to draw on the accomplishments of Christ. Paul essentially says, "In light of the blessings God has already blessed you with, in light of His provision for your armor, go ahead and claim your authority through prayer." To put it another way, without prayer, you don't get to use the things God has granted you.

Of course, the essence or heart of prayer is communication with God. I define prayer as relational communication with God. It is earthly permission for heavenly intervention. And since prayer is communication with God, we need to know something about Him. We need to understand His greatness. Many believers pray to a God who is too small. By their lack of understanding about God and their failure to appropriate His power, they reduce God to a micro-force in their lives. If your God is small, your prayers are going to be small. And if your prayers are small, you're a big target for the enemy.

Some of us spend hours a day talking with other people and only a minute talking with God. There's nothing wrong with talking to people. But people aren't the source of our spiritual authority. It's through prayer that we access our great God.

Knowing the God we are praying to also involves the understanding that prayer is not some magical formula by which we make God appear to do our bidding. God is not our genie. Some people have the idea that prayer is simply persuading God to do what we want Him to do. But prayer is not getting God to conform to us. Prayer is conforming ourselves to God's rightful rule over all.

It's fine to make our requests known to God. But we had better be sure that what we want God to do for us is what He wants to do for us. Otherwise, we will waste a lot of time and energy in prayer. If our knowledge of God is anemic, our prayers will be as well.

One of the best examples of a believer approaching God in prayer is the prayer of the prophet Daniel (Dan. 9:1–19). Daniel knew from his knowledge of Jeremiah's prophecy (v. 2) that the seventy years of Israel's captivity were about to end. So Daniel proceeded to pray a great prayer in which he confessed his people's sins and called on God to remember His covenant with Israel and end His people's humiliation in exile from Jerusalem. In other words, Daniel prayed God's own Word back to Him and called on Him to honor it.

One of the great things about prayer, especially if you know the Word of God, is that in prayer you can hold God to His Word. I don't mean you can coerce Him, but you can pray like Daniel, "O Lord, hear! O Lord, forgive! O Lord, listen and take action! For Your own sake, O my God, do not delay, because Your city and Your people are called by Your name" (v. 19). Daniel was reminding God of what He had said about Jerusalem and its people. He was holding God to His Word. Moses did the same thing when God announced He wanted to destroy Israel and start over with Moses (Exod. 32:10). Moses went before the Lord and reminded Him of three things: that these were the people God had rescued from Egypt; that if He destroyed the nation, the Egyptians would accuse God of doing evil; of His great promises to Abraham and his descendants (vv. 11–13).

Then verse 14 says, "The Lord changed His mind." God was still sovereign in this situation; but from our human standpoint, the intercession of Moses caused God to change His plans. Moses knew how to pray. He basically said, "God, if You do this, Your name is going to look bad, and You will be embarrassed among the gods. God, it is in Your best interest to preserve Your people. You need to forgive Your people." I call this putting God on the spot. Moses was able to do this in his prayer because he understood God's nature. Moses appealed to God's grace, knowing that His grace could overrule His wrath. But Moses had to pray before God would relent. In His sovereignty, God decided that He would allow Moses's prayer to "change His mind."

We have the same privilege as Moses to hold God to His Word in prayer. It's not a matter of His reluctance to fulfill His Word, but a test of our faith to believe and act on His Word. That fact has some tremendous implications for our spiritual warfare. For example, if the devil has been holding you in bondage to a habit you don't believe you can break, you need to hit him with the truth of Philippians 4:13: "I can do all things through Him who strengthens me." When you act in Christ, you have power.

The enemy has got us believing lies: "I can't overcome this habit." "There is no saving this marriage." "I can't be the spouse God wants me to be." If these things are really true, then God is a liar. We would never call God a liar, but that's what we do by our actions when we don't claim His Word and His power in prayer. In prayer, we can hold God to His Word.

Prayer is essential. When you pray properly, you wage warfare properly as well, and God puts out a restraining order against the spirits of darkness. Prayer gains you access to the full use of the armor God has supplied you as a warrior in His kingdom.

10

Winning the Battle

When the struggling British artist Jack Blackburn moved into an abandoned apartment just outside of London nearly two decades ago, *The Telegraph* reported his friends thought he had lost his mind. The dilapidated apartment wasn't livable at the time. But even without a deed to the property, Jack invested his own personal funds to plaster the walls, fix the plumbing, and make the place his home.

Thirteen years passed before the authorities noticed that the property, owned by another (the government), was being occupied by someone else. When they approached Jack to have him evicted, though, they ran into what is known as "squatter's rights." Because Jack had lived in the location for such a length of time, and because he had increased its value through upkeep and regular maintenance, the government was unable to evict him. Due to the civil matter of squatter's rights, the building was now his own. He had taken it by virtue of an elongated possession.

In America, seven years is often the length of time designated for someone to claim ownership by squatting. But regardless, there have been notable cases where people have broken a lock and entered a property to live in it for months on end and without paying rent. One of the more famous situations happened in Boca Raton, Florida, where squatters set their sights high and began inhabiting a $2.5 million mansion which had been foreclosed on by the bank. They lived there rent-free for nearly half a year.

Satan doesn't mind using this approach when it comes to gaining ground in the spiritual battle we are all in. We don't call it squatting when referring to Satan and his demons. We call it "strongholds."

A stronghold comes from the word meaning "fortress." A spiritual stronghold is a fortified area of our lives where Satan has taken residency, set up camp, and erected walls like a fortress. Strongholds can involve any number of things, such as emotional strongholds—including anxiety, bitterness, apathy, entitlement, and greed. Strongholds might also be more tangible in nature, such as drugs, pornography, or materialism. Whatever the specific stronghold might be, it is established when Satan has staked his claim to your thoughts, emotions, and actions. What's more, he has done so for so long that breaking free from his grasp, or evicting him as in the case of a squatter, becomes increasingly difficult with time.

Knowing how to break free is critical for living a life of victory in warfare. Let's close out our time together examining this approach to overcoming strongholds in our personal, family, church, and community lives.

WINNING IN YOUR PERSONAL LIFE

Remember Your Position in Christ

The first thing you must do if you want to experience victory in your personal life is to remember your position in Christ. We have seen that as believers, we have an exalted position—raised from the dead with Christ and seated with Him in the heavenly places (Eph. 2:6). And Paul spells out the corollary action that should follow this knowledge in another letter: "Therefore if you have been raised up with Christ, keep seeking the things above, where Christ is, seated at the right hand of God. Set your mind on the things above, not on the things that are on earth" (Col. 3:1–2). This means that if your mind is set on an earthly solution to your spiritual struggles, then you won't see a heavenly response. The solution to the strongholds Satan builds in our lives is found in Christ, "for in Him all the fullness of Deity dwells in bodily form, and in Him you have been made complete, and He is the head over all rule and authority" (Col. 2:9–10).

Christ has all the spiritual authority you will ever need because He is in charge of the universe. He has already beaten Satan and made a public spectacle of him (Col. 2:15). Therefore, if you are going to beat the evil one in your day-to-day life, you need to connect to Jesus, the One who has already won the victory over Satan. Your exalted position in Christ gives you not only a vital connection to Him, but also legal authority over Satan so that when he attacks you, you can announce, "Satan no longer has any rights or jurisdiction in my life." To do so means relying on God's provision.

The apostle James writes, "[God] gives a greater grace. Therefore it says, 'God is opposed to the proud, but gives grace to the humble'" (James 4:6).

What is this "greater grace" that God gives us? James is not talking about salvation here, so the issue isn't saving grace. This is the grace we need to live victorious lives as believers, the grace that is greater than the mess you may be in right now. It doesn't matter how big the mess is or what you've been through; the grace that is available to you in Christ is bigger than your mess.

Surrender to God

If all this grace is available, the natural question is, "How do we get it?" James lines out the answer in the following verses. He begins by saying, "Submit therefore to God" (4:7a). Before we get to what it means to submit to God, notice that James gives us a great picture of what submission does not mean (4:1–5). You're not submitted to God if your life is marked by things like illicit pleasure, strife, lust, envying, and friendship with the world.

If you want to submit to God so you can receive His greater grace, you need to understand all that is involved in submission. Submission is usually presented as the process of making a commitment to Christ. That's important, but it's possible to make a commitment to the Lord without really surrendering our wills to Him. Someone who's struggling with a stronghold might say, "I've made a commitment to the Lord, and I'm going to stop doing what I've been doing."

That sounds fine, but many people who make that kind of commitment promptly go out and fall flat on their faces. Why? Because commitment doesn't work unless it is preceded by surrender. A commitment may simply be another way of saying, "I'm going to do this myself. I'm going to beat this problem. I promised God I was going to do it, and I'm going to do it."

But we already know that we can't beat Satan on our own. So while commitment often says, "I can," surrender says, "Lord, I can't do this in my power. I'm too weak. I cannot live up to Your standards in my own strength."

When a soldier surrenders in a war, he is saying, "I quit. I can't fight any longer." If you want greater grace from God, you must surrender yourself and your own efforts to win the battle and tear down your strongholds. That's a different kind of surrender because you are surrendering to your Commander rather than to the enemy!

You may be thinking, *Wait a minute, Tony. In the previous chapter, you said believers needed to quit saying, "I can't."* Now you're saying we need to say, "I can't." What I'm talking about here is the attitude that says, "I can kick this thing myself." There's a big difference between that and realizing that we need Christ's strength to do what we need to do (Phil. 4:13). When it comes to what Christ can empower us to do, there's no reason to say we can't do something. But Christ's power doesn't kick in until we let go of our delusions of self-power. And that comes through surrender.

Repent of Sin

Along with remembering our position and relying on God's provision, tearing down our personal strongholds also involves repentance of sin. The apostle James continues in James 4:8–9, "Cleanse your hands, you sinners; and purify your hearts, you double-minded. Be miserable and mourn and weep; let your laughter be turned into mourning and your joy to gloom." James could not have been clearer about our need to call sin what it is and deal with it ruthlessly and completely. The reason God can't help some people is that they think they never sin. They believe they just "make mistakes." But Jesus didn't die for our mistakes. He died for our sins.

Admitting our sin simply means taking personal responsibility for it. If you don't see a stronghold as any big deal, you aren't going to be motivated to cleanse your hands and purify your heart of it. It takes humility to admit your sin, but when you humble yourself in this way, you get God's greater grace (James 4:6).

This is the difference between trying to take down those strongholds in your own strength and surrendering to God so He can empower you to do it. When God exalts you, you can rise above any problem, addiction, attachment, or anything else holding you captive.

We know what successful resistance looks like because we have the perfect example in the temptation of Jesus Christ (Matt. 4:1–11). Satan told Jesus, "You're hungry. A body has to eat. Go ahead and make Yourself some bread." "You deserve to win the attention of the people. Go ahead and jump." "You can have these kingdoms right now. Just bow down to me."

I can guarantee you that nothing you and I will ever face will compare with the temptations Jesus faced. And He answered every one of them with the Word of God: "It is written . . ." After Jesus used the Word on Satan, Satan left Him (Matt. 4:11). When you resist the devil with the Word of God, you pull out the lion's teeth.

So when Satan tells you, "You'll never really change," you can tell him, "I'm a new creation in Christ Jesus. I have been raised with Christ. I am setting my mind on things above, not on things below" (see 2 Cor. 5:17; Eph. 2:6; Col. 3:1). The next time Satan lies to you and says, "You'll never be free of your problem," tell him, "You're a liar, because God said anyone whom Jesus has set free is free indeed" (see John 8:36). Remind the devil that God's Word is truth (John 17:17) and that the truth sets people free (John 8:32). Satan will leave you alone, because he can't stand up to the Word.

WINNING IN YOUR FAMILY LIFE

It's safe to say that you know at least one family that either has fallen apart, is falling apart, or is functioning far below what God intended the family to be. The family you know may even be yours. Some families suffer because the relationship between the husband and wife has become paralyzed. Other families are hurting because rebellious children are causing grief. And other families are suffering because some members are reaping a harvest of trouble from the sins committed by an earlier generation.

All these problems and more can easily become strongholds that Satan builds to get a grip on a family and keep it from being everything God intended the family to be. The tragedy is that many families battling satanic strongholds decide that the fight is no longer worth the grief, so they want to give up. Spouses head for divorce court because they don't see any solution to their problem.

Satan is definitely in a "building boom" today in erecting family strongholds. He knows what he is doing because he has been at it for a long time. So how does Satan work his way into a family and build his strongholds? I'm not just talking about a family having an occasional argument or some other conflict. I'm talking about a situation in which a family is imprisoned by a problem from which it can't break free. Satan uses a number of means to break down a family and build strongholds. One way is through unresolved anger. As we see in Ephesians 4:26–27: "Be angry, and yet do not sin; do not let the sun go down on your anger, and do not give the devil an opportunity."

There are lots of angry people out there—angry at parents, friends, children, or even themselves. If a wrong has been committed against you, you have a right to be angry. The Bible says that the Lord is angry with the wicked every day (Psalm 7:11 KJV). Anger at sin is valid. But prolonged anger violates the scriptural command to resolve it quickly, and it provides the ground Satan needs to build that unresolved anger into a stronghold. Paul says it clearly in

Ephesians 4:27. Lingering anger becomes an opportunity for Satan. It gives the enemy the unlocked door he needs to enter your home and destroy the place. For some of us, not only has the sun gone down on our anger, but the moon has gone down as well. This kind of anger makes everyone else in the family pay for what one or two people have done.

Rebellion is another powerful weapon Satan uses to disrupt families and build strongholds. Rebellion simply means to go against God's established order of authority. Satan was the original rebel, so it's not surprising that he would attempt to foment rebellion in the family. Rebellious children can tear a family apart as quickly as anything. So can adults who refuse to submit themselves to God's legitimate chain of command.

In fact, I want to spend most of my time here dealing with the adults because God said in Exodus 20:5 that He would pass the results of disobedience on to the third and fourth generation. Parents can hand their children and grandchildren a real mess when they rebel against God's authority. Some Christians are setting in motion a pattern of rebellion that will have generational consequences if the pattern is not reversed.

The apostle Peter has some strong words about rebellion as it relates to the angelic conflict and then to people who have joined in that rebellion against God. Peter writes, "God did not spare angels when they sinned, but cast them into hell and committed them to pits of darkness, reserved for judgment" (2 Peter 2:4). The sin of these angels was that they joined Satan in his rebellion. The people of Noah's day,

and the citizens of Sodom and Gomorrah, can also be classi-
fied as rebels. Peter reminds us that God also brought judgment against the world of Noah's day and against Sodom and
Gomorrah (vv. 5–6). Then Peter says, "The Lord knows how
. . . to keep the unrighteous under punishment for the day of
judgment" (v. 9).

But then in verses 10–12, Peter applies the principle of
God's judgment to the false teachers of his day. Notice a few
traits of these people. They "indulge the flesh in its corrupt
desires," "despise authority," and are "self-willed." They are
also not afraid to "revile angelic majesties" (v. 10). What
is the fate of these rebels? They are like wild, unreasoning
animals, "born as creatures of instinct to be captured and
killed" (v. 12). That's strong talk! These false teachers had
no respect for God or His holy angels. They refused to place
themselves under divine or angelic authority, and therefore
they placed themselves under God's severe judgment.

My point is that wherever you see rebellion against God's
legitimate chain of command, you find God's judgment and
not God's help. If a husband and father is rebelling against
the authority of Christ in his life and home, he can't blame
God if his family is falling apart. To get things back on track,
he must line himself up under God's established chain of authority. In connection with this, let me remind you again of
a seminal passage, 1 Corinthians 11:3–10. Verse 3 outlines
God's chain of authority: "I want you to understand that
Christ is the head of every man, and the man is the head of a
woman, and God is the head of Christ."

This issue of obedience to proper authority even applies

to Jesus Christ, because He is under the authority of His Father. Every Christian man is under the authority of Christ, and every wife is under the authority of her husband. This is the way God intended things to be in the church and in the home.

Rebellion is a serious sin in God's sight. It can lead to the presence of satanic strongholds. There's only one way to deal with rebellion and that's to remove it like a cancer, no matter how radical the procedure required to get it out.

With that in mind, let's look at one of the most potent weapons you can use to tear down satanic strongholds in your family: honoring God-ordained roles. The strength of the family begins with the strength of the marriage bond. And God has a lot to say about that. I've counseled thousands of couples over four decades of serving as a pastor, and this is the preeminent issue that shows up time and again: either one or both of them have stepped outside of the God-ordained role.

Paul writes, "Wives, be subject to your husbands, as is fitting in the Lord" (Col. 3:18). Put another way, "Wives, honor your husband's position of headship." A wife may say, "But I don't like my husband right now." You don't have to like him to honor the position God has put him in. A lot of people don't like their boss, but they honor their boss's position. God calls a wife to honor her husband, whether or not she agrees with him all the time. Sarah is the model of this honor, because she called Abraham "lord" (1 Peter 3:6). And what did Sarah get? She got a miracle, a baby when she was ninety years old. God miraculously intervened in Sarah's life and gave her Isaac, a miracle child. Peter says that when a woman operates this way, it is precious in the sight of God.

Why is this a big deal with God? First, because it reflects the order He has established. And second, because we are talking about spiritual warfare and satanic strongholds. Satan is so potent that even the archangel Michael didn't rebuke him. We need the weapons of God to defeat the devil.

The Bible also addresses husbands. It takes two to tango, and the husband is just as responsible for remaining in proper alignment under Jesus Christ as his wife is under him. More often than not, it is the husband that fails to honor this role, which then leads to chaos in the home as the rebellion trickles down to everyone else. Husbands, you cannot blame your wife for not following your leadership when you are not following Christ's. Scripture says, "Husbands, love your wives, and do not be embittered against them" (Col. 3:19). We also read,

> Husbands, love your wives, just as Christ also loved the church and gave Himself up for her, so that He might sanctify her, having cleansed her by the washing of water with the word, that He might present to Himself the church in all her glory, having no spot or wrinkle or any such thing; but that she would be holy and blameless. So husbands ought also to love their own wives as their own bodies. He who loves his own wife loves himself; for no one ever hated his own flesh, but nourishes and cherishes it, just as Christ also does the church. (Eph. 5:25–29)

When you view your role in that perspective, kingdom men, being a husband takes on a whole new definition. No longer will you think your wife exists to simply grant your wishes. Your wife is your partner, not your servant. How can you know, Christian husband, if you are loving your wife? It's simple. What are you sacrificing for her? Loving your wife like Christ loved the church always involves sacrifice.

In Nehemiah 4:14, this great leader told the people of Jerusalem, who were being threatened by their enemies, "Fight for your brothers, your sons, your daughters, your wives and your houses." That's what we have been talking about all along. We're in a spiritual war, although some of us haven't started fighting with God's weapons yet. When you're at war, you can't afford to let the enemy build strongholds in your backyard.

WINNING IN YOUR CHURCH LIFE

The Bible is clear that Satan can build his strongholds in the lives of individuals and families. But he can also gain ground in the church of Jesus Christ and erect strongholds that hinder the work of God. Bringing spiritual warfare inside the doors of the church is a key strategy of the devil. He knows if he can weaken the church internally, he can weaken its witness and impact on the world.

How do we tear down strongholds in the church? The place to begin is with the Lord and Head of the church and His message to the people who make up His body. In the opening chapters of Revelation, we meet the risen Jesus Christ in all of

His power and glory. There is no reducing this person to a safe, easy-to-manage, milquetoast Lord who is a threat to no one. On the contrary, the apostle John saw a vision of Jesus Christ standing among His church, wearing the robes of judge and priest. His voice sounded like "many waters" (Rev. 1:15). He was thunderous in His statements. A two-edged sword came out of His mouth (v. 16). In fact, when John saw Jesus, he "fell at His feet like a dead man" (v. 17).

The Lord whom John saw had a message concerning the future, and that is the bulk of the Revelation. But Jesus also had a message for the present, to His church. He told John, "Write in a book what you see, and send it to the seven churches" (Rev. 1:11).

In the Bible, seven is the number of perfection or completion. So even though Jesus' message was for seven real churches in Asia Minor, it was also His complete message to all churches in this age.

A Message About Love

The first message is to the church at Ephesus, and it is one of love:

> I know your deeds and your toil and perseverance, and that you cannot tolerate evil men, and you put to the test those who call themselves apostles, and they are not, and you found them to be false; and you have perseverance and have endured for My name's sake, and have not grown weary. But I have this against you, that you have left your first love. (2:2–4)

The first lesson of the risen Christ to His church is that if we want to see His power and authority operating in our midst, we must never let programs replace our passion for Him. The church at Ephesus had a great program. This church believed all the right things. They had doctrinal soundness. Truth was present, but it was truth devoid of love.

It is possible for the church to have all the right answers and still fail the test. The church can be doctrinally correct and yet spiritually dead when it loses sight of Christ. It's necessary to have correct doctrine. But correct doctrine ought to help us love Christ more. It's right to take a stand for the truth. But the truth should make us more passionate to know Christ intimately.

The city of Ephesus was dominated by the temple and the worship of the goddess Diana, so the demonic world was very active in Ephesus. In this pagan environment, God's people needed to keep their love for Him strong. So do we in our evil environment. This issue of first love for the Savior is so important that Christ saw its lack as a sin to be repented of. Failure to do so would mean that Christ would remove His presence from the church (2:5).

A Message About Faithfulness

The second church Jesus addressed was the church in Smyrna. To these believers, Jesus says,

> "I know your tribulation and your poverty (but you are rich), and the blasphemy by those who say they are Jews and are not, but are a synagogue of Satan. Do not

fear what you are about to suffer. Behold, the devil is
about to cast some of you into prison, so that you will
be tested, and you will have tribulation for ten days. Be
faithful until death, and I will give you the crown of life."
(2:9–10)

This was a message concerning faithfulness. The believers in Smyrna were going through hard times. Many of them
were poor, and they were facing persecution by a group of
people energized by Satan. It would've been easy for the
church in Smyrna to throw in the towel and let Satan have
the victory he sought.

A lot of people are willing to follow Jesus as long as they
are getting Christmas blessings. Everybody likes a God who
gives out goodies, who simply invites people to "name it and
claim it." But Jesus has called us to take up our cross and
follow Him (Mark 8:34). A cross is an instrument of suffering. We can't follow Jesus only during the good times and
call ourselves the church. We must be faithful to Him even
when following Him involves suffering. When times are
good, they are good because God is good. But even when
times are bad, God is still good.

The church's job is to obey Christ faithfully, not to please
everybody. The church is not on earth to win friends and
influence people. If it's a choice between standing for Christ
and winning popularity, there's only one choice the church
can make. We are called to be faithful no matter what, and
when we do that, Jesus will take care of the rest.

A Message About Compromise

The third church the risen Lord sent a message to was the church in Pergamum:

> "I know where you dwell, where Satan's throne is; and you hold fast My name, and did not deny My faith even in the days of Antipas, My witness, My faithful one, who was killed among you, where Satan dwells. But I have a few things against you, because you have there some who hold the teaching of Balaam, who kept teaching Balak to put a stumbling block before the sons of Israel, to eat things sacrificed to idols and to commit acts of immorality. So you also have some who in the same way hold the teaching of the Nicolaitans." (2:13–15)

"Satan's throne" was a reference to the throne of Zeus, which was on a hill in Pergamum. Jesus called it Satan's throne because behind every idol or false god is a demon. Pergamum was another city in which Satan was having a field day in terms of spiritual warfare. The church at Pergamum held to its witness even when one of its members was martyred for Christ. But the church was also compromising with the enemy by tolerating false teachers in its midst. This was a spiritual warfare issue because false teachers are energized ultimately by Satan.

When the church allows people to teach false doctrine, it puts a stumbling block in the path of God's people. Satan can build some mighty strongholds in a church where the people are being led by a false teacher to commit acts of immorality and defile the worship of God. The church must address compromise when it occurs because God has called us to a higher standard. The church is to be visibly different from the world. The church's first call is not to try to be relevant. Its first call is to be biblical.

A Message About Holiness

The Lord's fourth message, to the church at Thyatira, gives us another side of this issue of dealing with sin in the church. This was a message about holiness:

> "I know your deeds, and your love and faith and service and perseverance, and that your deeds of late are greater than at first. But I have this against you, that you tolerate the woman Jezebel, who calls herself a prophetess, and she teaches and leads My bond-servants astray so that they commit acts of immorality and eat things sacrificed to idols." (2:19–20)

Like the other churches, the church at Thyatira had some good things going for it. The people had grown in their faith and love and service to the Lord. But the church had a major problem in its midst: a woman the Lord called Jezebel. That may not have been this woman's actual name, but in using the name Jezebel, Jesus was drawing on the image of Israel's wicked, conniving, domineering queen who manipulated her husband, King Ahab, and everyone else. Jezebel ran the show. This woman had theologized her rebellion by giving herself the title "prophetess." But that only masked her sin.

No one was dealing with the problem; no one was speaking out against her rebellion and sin. She claimed to be spiritually gifted, and the authentic leadership of the church wasn't calling her on it. It's pretty easy for Satan to build a stronghold in the church when the church invites his kids inside and gives them a hammer and nails. This church may have tolerated Jezebel, but God didn't tolerate her. She and her followers were under His judgment (2:21-23a).

The church cannot tolerate unholiness, because God will not tolerate it. There were people in Thyatira who had remained faithful to God and had not followed Jezebel (v. 24). But when evil is tolerated in the church, it spreads and infects the whole body the way a little bit of yeast spreads through a whole loaf of bread (1 Cor. 5:6).

A Message About Progress

Sardis was another church with major problems. In fact, there were only a few people in the entire church who had not "soiled their garments" and were therefore worthy to "walk with [Christ] in white" (Rev. 3:4). To the rest, Jesus sent this message:

> "I know your deeds, that you have a name that you are alive, but you are dead. Wake up, and strengthen the things that remain, which were about to die; for I have not found your deeds completed in the sight of My God. So remember what you have received and heard; and

keep it, and repent. Therefore if you do not wake up,
I will come like a thief, and you will not know at what
hour I will come to you." (3:1–3)

Jesus was addressing a sleeping church that had made
no spiritual progress worth talking about. It's hard to move
forward when you're asleep. Why do some churches fail to
make progress? One reason is that they are living off what
God did yesterday. Watch out for a church where all the
people can talk about is what God did in the good old days,
how things used to be around there. The church at Sardis
didn't have much left, and even the things that remained
were about to go belly-up. This church was stuck.

The problem with this, of course, is that you can't stand
still in the spiritual life. You are either moving forward, or
you're moving backward. There is no such thing as coasting
in neutral. Living in the past is like trying to drive while star-
ing in the rearview mirror of your car. You move forward by
focusing on the windshield, not the rearview mirror. Notice
how large your windshield is compared to your rearview
mirror. The windshield covers a lot more territory because
the object of driving is to move forward. You only need to
glance back every once in a while to avoid making a mistake
while you're moving forward.

Satan wants to keep the church focused on the rearview
mirror of yesterday so we won't pay attention to where we're
going today. Jesus says, "Wake up, open your eyes, and move
on to tomorrow."

A Message About Obedience

The church at Philadelphia was the church Jesus commended so highly. He had nothing negative to say about this faithful church. And yet, Satan was there trying to gain a foothold:

> "I know your deeds. . . . You have a little power, and have
> kept My word, and have not denied My name. Behold,
> I will cause those of the synagogue of Satan, who say
> that they are Jews and are not, but lie—I will make
> them come and bow down at your feet, and make them
> know that I have loved you. Because you have kept the
> word of My perseverance, I also will keep you from the
> hour of testing, that hour which is about to come upon
> the whole world, to test those who dwell on the earth."
> (3:8–10)

This church kept God's Word even though Satan was harassing the believers through the people in one of his "synagogues." Satan was trying to build a stronghold in the church, but the people wouldn't allow it.

Notice that the secret to this church's success wasn't its great power. "You have a little power," Jesus told them. The key was that they kept His Word and did not deny His name. When the church is obedient to Christ, He will take care of Satan. But if we deny Him, He will deny us.

One reason we don't see more prayers answered in the church is that so many believers basically deny Christ by their actions all week. They don't acknowledge that they know Him; but come Sunday, they're ready to hear from Him. The best preventive for Satan's work in the church is obedience to the Word of God.

A Message About Commitment

The seventh and final church the risen Lord addressed was the church of Laodicea.

Laodicea was a wealthy Roman city. The church was rich too, and the people were really with it. This was "the church of what's happening now." But it was also very sick:

> "I know your deeds, that you are neither cold nor hot;
> I wish that you were cold or hot. So because you are
> lukewarm, and neither hot nor cold, I will spit you out
> of My mouth. Because you say, 'I am rich, and have
> become wealthy, and have need of nothing,' and you do
> not know that you are wretched and miserable and poor
> and blind and naked." (3:15–17)

This is one that really hits home for a lot of us. There is nothing wrong with being financially successful, if your success is the result of God's blessing on your honest efforts. But the church at Laodicea reminds us that it's possible to become too successful. And when that happens, Satan has some good ground on which to build a stronghold.

How do you know when you've become too successful? You've become too successful when your focus on the blessings of God in your life has replaced the presence and power of God in your life. If you have more today than you have ever had before, and yet God has less of you than He has ever had before, you are a Laodicean Christian.

Laodicea was a garment-making center, so the people had fine clothes. But spiritually, they were naked. They also made an eye ointment in Laodicea, but the church there was spiritually blind. The Laodiceans needed to make a few purchases, but not with money. They needed spiritual gold, garments of righteousness, and the eye salve of the Holy Spirit. These are things that money just can't buy. The trouble was, the church of Laodicea had already moved to a better neighborhood, and Christ wasn't welcome there. Satan had a stronghold built there, but the Lord of the church was shut out. It was now up to each member to welcome Christ. So even if your church is not responding collectively to Christ, you can still respond individually and enter into intimate fellowship with Him.

WINNING IN YOUR COMMUNITY LIFE

When we talk about satanic strongholds in the community, we're talking about strongholds that could affect government, education, or the private corporate world. The Bible teaches that Satan is in control of the institutions of this world, so his influence can be seen in every sphere. Colossians 1:16 says that through Christ, God created all things, "both in the heavens and on earth, visible and invisible, whether thrones or dominions or rulers or authorities—all things have been created through Him and for Him."

We looked at this verse earlier, but let's slow down and

study it once more. Paul says the four entities he names were created both in heaven and on earth. So there are heavenly thrones, in other words, and there are earthly thrones. The same is true of dominions, rulers, and authorities. This means that behind the thrones, dominions, rulers, and authorities we see on earth are thrones, dominions, rulers, and authorities in the heavenly realm. If you want to tear down strongholds in any of these categories on earth, you must be able to address the problem from the standpoint of heaven. Let me define the four terms Paul uses in Colossians 1:16 because they are societal in nature. They have to do with the community, the world around us.

A *throne* is a chair of authority. Kings and queens sit on thrones. America doesn't have a throne, but we have a chair of authority. It's the executive chair the president occupies in the Oval Office of the White House.

A *dominion* is the territory that is ruled by the authority on the throne. America's dominion includes the fifty states and the territories our nation rules around the world.

The third term Paul uses in Colossians 1:16 is *rulers*. A ruler is a specific person who occupies a place of authority, whether that person be the mayor, the governor, the president, the chairman of the board, the king or queen, or whatever. Rulers sit on thrones to rule their dominions.

The fourth term is *authorities*. These are the rules, laws, traditions, or sanctions that legitimize the throne. In the case of America, our authority is the Constitution. It is the governing document by which the rulers rule.

These are the four areas or categories by which life here

on earth is organized. What we need to understand is that these entities were created by God, but since government was instituted after the fall, it is subject to the same spiritual disorders as the rest of creation. Evil people are still responsible for the evil they do, but what I want us to see is that institutional, structural evil is not just accidental or random. There's a plan operating behind the throne.

Therefore, if there is a problem with government or any other sphere of life, ranting and raving and posting or tweeting about the people we're up against is not the first thing we need to do. The first thing to do is to get heaven acting on our behalf. Satan seeks to control a community through its institutions. Therefore, human institutions have a spiritual dimension to them. This is why there can be structural evil, systemic evil, corporate evil, as well as individual evil. And yet, as we saw earlier, the Bible says that Jesus Christ created these entities. This means that business, government, and education as created by God are good. It's the intrusion of sin into the structures of this world, as well as the people of this world, that causes what God meant for good to be used for evil. Satan builds his strongholds in a community through people and institutions that are influenced by the evil one.

That's why the church must attack institutional and structural evil, just as it attacks other forms of evil, if it wants to have maximum impact in our communities. The power to tear down strongholds on an institutional level is the same power we draw on to tear down personal, family, and church strongholds. It's the power of Jesus Christ. Therefore, by virtue of Jesus' victory, the thrones, dominions, rulers, and authorities mentioned in Colossians 1:16 no longer have the final say. Jesus has overcome them and rendered them powerless.

Remember, we're not saying that human institutions are totally evil. Romans 13:1 says the powers that exist are ordained by God. But the Bible clearly teaches that the systems of this unregenerate world are under Satan's power: "The whole world lies in the power of the evil one" (1 John 5:19).

In fact, instead of writing off our community structures as hopeless, we need to put committed Christians in places of authority where they can bring the righteous rule of Jesus Christ to bear on these institutions. If Christ has conquered the thrones and dominions of this world, we ought to see His victory being reflected in the way our communities function.

Someone may ask, "Since Christ has already defeated Satan, why doesn't He just go ahead and wipe out all the evil and set up His rule on earth? Why do we have to put up with all this mess?" Someday, Jesus is going to come back physically and establish His worldwide rule. But until then, He wants us to wrestle against the principalities and powers. Why? The church is the vehicle through which God has chosen to demonstrate His authority in this age. In other words, the Head of the church has done His part. He has disarmed Satan and given us all the power and spiritual authority we need. Now He wants His body to do its part, to take His victory into every sphere of human life and demonstrate His authority over it.

This is why Paul prayed that we would know "the sur-passing greatness of His power toward us who believe" (Eph. 1:19). Paul went on to explain that power:

> [This is the power] which He brought about in Christ, when He raised Him from the dead and seated Him at His right hand in the heavenly places, far above all rule and authority and power and dominion, and every name that is named, not only in this age but also in the one to come. And He put all things in subjection under His feet, and gave Him as head over all things to the church, which is His body, the fullness of Him who fills all in all. (vv. 20–23)

We are God's delivery service, taking God's solution to a sick society.

This ought to raise a question in our minds. Since the church is armed with God's authority, and since Satan and his forces have been disarmed and humiliated, why aren't we seeing Christ's victory being reproduced on earth? Why aren't the thrones and rulers and dominions of this earth recognizing the authority of Christ?

There can be only one answer. The church is not doing its job. The body of Christ is not obeying its Head. Our assign-ment is to carry out what has been accomplished by Christ on the cross by comprehensively applying all of God's truth to all of life.

If our communities are going over to the enemy, it's be-cause the church is spending too much time within its own walls and not infiltrating society. Such passivity is often made possible by a defeatist theology that uses the imminent return of Christ as an excuse for not seeking cultural transformation. We must seek to disciple the nations while simultaneously looking for the return of Christ.

Our job as the church is explained in Ephesians 3:10. Paul writes, "That the manifold wisdom of God might now be made known through the church to the rulers and the authorities in the heavenly places." The church's job is to advertise, manifest, and work out the victory of Jesus Christ here on earth. The church is to display God's wisdom and victory in warfare to the spiritual realm itself. That means we must want to make a difference in this satanically controlled, sinful world. It means we don't want our communities held hostage by evil people. It means we want to see the righteousness of Jesus Christ permeate every area of life.

Elsewhere, Paul tells us where to begin in demonstrating Jesus' victory on earth: "*First of all*, then, I urge that entreaties and prayers, petitions and thanksgivings, be made on behalf of all men, for kings and all who are in authority" (1 Tim. 2:1–2a, emphasis added). Paul tells Timothy, "First of all, pray." If we could get believers to respond to calls for prayer the way they respond to other Christian events and programs, the church would be way too much for Satan to handle. Why? Prayer engages the heavenlies. Paul understood that if you really want to see things change, the first person you have to talk to is God. If we want to see Satan's strongholds in the community come down, the church needs to go to prayer "for kings and all who are in authority." We should pray for the redemption of earthly authorities. And even if they do not come to Christ, we are urged to pray that God might still influence them for good so that we will live tranquil lives. In other words, the church's prayer life should be so powerful that it helps to shape society.

Could it be that we are not seeing more of God's movement in society because rather than praying first, the church is praying as a last resort? To be sure, our prayers must be married to righteous activism that seeks to tear down the evil in community structures. Without action, there is no evidence that we are praying in faith (James 2:17). However, the most dedicated activity in the world won't go very far unless it is rooted in prayer.

Paul also says back in 1 Timothy 2:1 that we should pray for "all men." Our prayers are not limited to those in power. We need to pray that all people will be saved. Everybody has some kind of impact on society. If you want to pray with power for unsaved people, ask them if they have any needs you can pray for. When you pray for the needs of unbelievers in order to help them, and help lead them to Christ, God is inclined to act because He desires all people to be saved. Here is a biblical formula for the kind of spiritual warfare praying that brings down satanic strongholds: there must be agreement and unity, we must come together in Jesus' name, and we need to focus on Him, bringing Him into the midst of our prayer circle. When we do that, and then act in light of God's comprehensive revealed Word, including the application of the revelatory aspects of biblical justice and love, we'll see prayers answered. We'll have power to affect the community that we never thought possible.

GAINING THE KINGDOM VICTORY

Let me close out our time together by showing you why God has you and me in His Kingdom in the first place. In Daniel 7:13–14, the prophet wrote:

> "I kept looking in the night visions,
> And behold, with the clouds of heaven
> One like a Son of Man was coming,
> And He came up to the Ancient of Days
> And was presented before Him.
> "And to Him was given dominion,
> Glory *and a kingdom*,
> That all the peoples, nations and men of every language
> Might serve Him.
> His dominion is an everlasting dominion
> Which will not pass away;
> And His kingdom is one
> Which will not be destroyed." (emphasis added)

You were brought into God's Kingdom to serve Him, to do His will, and to confiscate from Satan that which belongs to God. You were brought here to be a warrior for the King, winning spiritual battle after spiritual battle for His glory.

This warfare you've been placed in is different from all

other wars, though. Above and beyond the difference of its sheer magnitude and scope is that this war is fought in a place none of us has ever seen. It is a cosmic conflict waged in the invisible, spiritual realm, which is simultaneously fleshed out in the context of the visible, physical realm.

As we have seen throughout the pages of this book, behind every physical disturbance, setback, ailment, or issue that you face is a spiritual root. Without first identifying and dealing with the root spiritual cause, attempts at fixing only the physical problem will provide a temporary solution at best. There is nothing that your five senses partake of within your physical being that is not first generated by that which your five senses do not partake of. In light of this truth, you and I need to engage a sixth sense—a spiritual sense—when fighting this war. We must employ that which goes beyond the obvious use of physiology and address the spiritual root before we can ever truly treat the physical symptoms.

One final thing to remember as you wage successful warfare is that the strength that you need to win in the battle with the devil has already been supplied to you by God. This is absolutely vital to remember. You already have all that you need to win this war. Your strength is not accumulated nor is it earned. It is supplied by the grace of God, who equips you to live the life to which you have been called.

Paul writes to us in the book of Ephesians, "Be strong in the Lord and in the strength of His might." Notice in the passage that Paul tells us to be *strong in the Lord*. In your humanity, you do not have the power to overcome angels— even fallen ones like the devil and his legions. God Himself is the only one capable of putting the devil in his place. He is the One who empowers you to achieve victory in your encounters with darkness because your victory rests in Him. He is the One who will enable you to truly win this spiritual battle.

Acknowledgments

I am extremely grateful to the Moody Publishers family for their partnership with me in the development of this project. Special thanks go to Greg Thornton who has been with me on this publishing journey with Moody Publishers from the start. I also want to thank Philip Rawley for his editorial work on the original manuscript, along with Kevin Emmert who had the vision to see this new book come to life. Many thanks to Connor Sterchi for his editorial expertise and to Heather Hair for her collaboration on this manuscript.

APPENDIX:

The Urban Alternative

The Urban Alternative (TUA) equips, empowers, and unites Christians to impact *individuals, families, churches,* and *communities* through a thoroughly kingdom agenda worldview. In teaching truth, we seek to transform lives.

The core cause of the problems we face in our personal lives, homes, churches, and societies is a spiritual one; therefore, the only way to address it is spiritually. We've tried a political, social, economic, and even a religious agenda.

It's time for a **Kingdom agenda**.

The Kingdom agenda can be defined as the visible manifestation of the comprehensive rule of God over every area of life.

The unifying central theme throughout the Bible is the glory of God and the advancement of His kingdom. The conjoining thread from Genesis to Revelation—from beginning to end—is focused on one thing: God's glory through advancing God's kingdom.

When you do not have that theme, the Bible becomes disconnected stories that are great for inspiration but seem to be unrelated in purpose and direction. The Bible exists to share God's movement in history toward the establishment and expansion of His kingdom highlighting the connectivity throughout which is the kingdom. Understanding that increases the relevancy of this several-thousand-year-old manuscript to your day-to-day living, because the kingdom is not only then, it is now.

The absence of the kingdom's influence in our personal and family lives, churches, and communities has led to a deterioration in our world of immense proportions:

- People live segmented, compartmentalized lives because they lack God's kingdom worldview.
- Families disintegrate because they exist for their own satisfaction rather than for the kingdom.
- Churches are limited in the scope of their impact because they fail to comprehend that the goal of the church is not the church itself, but the kingdom.

- Communities have nowhere to turn to find real solutions for real people who have real problems because the church has become divided, ingrown, and unable to transform the cultural landscape in any relevant way.

The kingdom agenda offers us a way to see and live life with a solid hope by optimizing the solutions of heaven. When God—and His rule—is no longer the final and authoritative standard under which all else falls, order and hope leaves with Him. But the reverse of that is true as well: as long as you have God, you have hope. If God is still in the picture, and as long as His agenda is still on the table, it's not over.

Even if relationships collapse, God will sustain you. Even if finances dwindle, God will keep you. Even if dreams die, God will revive you. As long as God—and His rule—is still the overarching rule in your life, family, church and community, there is always hope.

Our world needs the King's agenda. Our churches need the King's agenda. Our families need the King's agenda. In many major cities, there is a loop that drivers can take when they want to get somewhere on the other side of the city, but don't necessarily want to head straight through downtown. This loop will take you close enough to the city so that you can see its towering buildings and skyline, but not close enough to actually experience it.

This is precisely what we, as a culture, have done with God. We have put Him on the "loop" of our personal, family, church, and community lives. He's close enough to be at hand should we need Him in an emergency, but far enough away that He can't be the center of who we are.

We want God on the "loop," not the King of the Bible who comes downtown into the very heart of our ways. Leaving God on the "loop" brings about dire consequences as we have seen in our own lives and with others. But when we make God and His rule the centerpiece of all we think, do or say, it is then that we will experience Him in the way He longs to be experienced by us.

He wants us to be kingdom people with kingdom minds set on fulfilling His kingdom's purposes. He wants us to pray, as Jesus did, "Not my will, but Thy will be done." Because His is the kingdom, the power, and the glory.

There is only one God, and we are not Him. As King and Creator, God calls the shots. It is only when we align ourselves underneath His comprehensive hand that we will access His full power and authority in all spheres of life: personal, familial, church, and community.

As we learn how to govern ourselves under God, we then transform the institutions of family, church, and society from a biblically based kingdom worldview.

Under Him, we touch heaven and change earth.

To achieve our goal, we use a variety of strategies, approaches, and resources for reaching and equipping as many people as possible.

BROADCAST MEDIA

Millions of individuals experience *The Alternative with Dr. Tony Evans* through the daily radio broadcast playing on nearly **1,200 radio outlets** and in over **130 countries**. The broadcast can also be seen on several television networks and is viewable online at TonyEvans.org. You can also listen or view the daily broadcast by downloading the Tony Evans app for free in the App store. Over 4,000,000 message downloads occur each year.

LEADERSHIP TRAINING

The Tony Evans Training Center (TETC) facilitates educational programming that embodies the ministry philosophy of Dr. Tony Evans as expressed through the kingdom agenda. The training courses focus on leadership development and discipleship in the following five tracks:

- Bible & Theology
- Personal Growth
- Family and Relationships

- Church Health and Leadership Development
- Society and Community Impact Strategies

The TETC program includes courses for both local and online students. Furthermore, TETC programming includes course work for non-student attendees. Pastors, Christian leaders, and Christian laity, both local and at a distance, can seek out The Kingdom Agenda Certificate for personal, spiritual, and professional development. Some courses are valued for CEU credit as well as viable in transferring for college credit with our partner school(s).

The Kingdom Agenda Pastors (KAP) provides a *viable network* for *like-minded pastors* who embrace the Kingdom Agenda philosophy. Pastors have the opportunity to go deeper with Dr. Tony Evans as they are given greater biblical knowledge, practical applications, and resources to impact individuals, families, churches, and communities. KAP welcomes *senior and associate pastors* of all churches. KAP also offers an annual Summit held each year in Dallas with intensive seminars, workshops, and resources.

Pastors' Wives Ministry, founded by Dr. Lois Evans, provides *counsel, encouragement,* and *spiritual resources* for pastors' wives as they serve with their husbands in the ministry. A primary focus of the ministry is the KAP Summit that offers senior pastors' wives a safe place to *reflect, renew,* and *relax* along with training in personal development, spiritual growth, and care for their emotional and physical well-being.

COMMUNITY IMPACT

National Church Adopt-A-School Initiative (NCAASI) prepares churches across the country to impact communities by using *public schools as the primary vehicle for effecting positive social change* in urban youth and families. Leaders of churches, school districts, faith-based organizations, and other nonprofit organizations are equipped with the knowledge and tools to *forge partnerships* and build *strong social service delivery systems.* This training is based on the comprehensive church-based community impact strategy conducted by Oak Cliff Bible Fellowship. It addresses such areas as economic development, education, housing, health revitalization, family renewal, and racial reconciliation. We assist churches in tailoring the model to meet specific needs of their communities while simultaneously addressing the spiritual and moral frame of reference. Training events are held annually in the Dallas area at Oak Cliff Bible Fellowship.

Athlete's Impact (AI) exists as an outreach both into and through the sports arena. Coaches are the most influential factor in young people's lives, even ahead of their parents. With the growing rise of fatherlessness in our culture, more young people are looking to their coaches for guidance, character development, practical needs, and hope. After coaches, athletes are next on the influencer scale. Athletes (whether professional or amateur) influence younger athletes and kids within their spheres of impact. Knowing this, we have made it our aim to equip and train coaches and athletes on how to live out and utilize their God-given roles for the benefit of the kingdom. We aim to do this through our iCoach App, weCoach Football Conference as well as resources such as *The Playbook: A Life Strategy Guide for Athletes*.

RESOURCE DEVELOPMENT

We are fostering lifelong learning partnerships with the people we serve by providing a variety of published materials. Dr. Evans has published more than 100 unique titles based on over 40 years of preaching, whether that is in booklet, book, or Bible study format. The goal is to strengthen individuals in their walk with God and service to others.

For more information and a complimentary copy of
Dr. Evans's devotional newsletter, call (800) 800-3222
or write TUA at P.O. Box 4000, Dallas TX 75208,
or visit us online at www.TonyEvans.org

Tony EVANS
THE URBAN ALTERNATIVE

YOUR *Eternity* IS OUR *Priority*

At The Urban Alternative, eternity is our priority—for the individual, the family, the church and the nation. The 45-year teaching ministry of Tony Evans has allowed us to reach a world in need with:

The Alternative – Our flagship radio program brings hope and comfort to an audience of millions on over 1,400 radio outlets across the country.

tonyevans.org – Our library of teaching resources provides solid Bible teaching through the inspirational books and sermons of Tony Evans.

Tony Evans Training Center – Experience the adventure of God's Word with our online classroom, providing at-your-own-pace courses for your PC or mobile device.

Tony Evans app – Packed with audio and video clips, devotionals, Scripture readings and dozens of other tools, the mobile app provides inspiration on-the-go.

**Explore God's kingdom today.
Live for more than the moment.**
Live for *eternity*.

tonyevans.org

WHERE HAVE ALL THE DISCIPLES GONE?

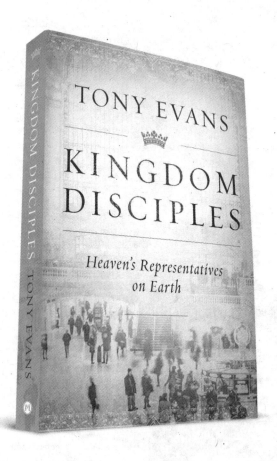

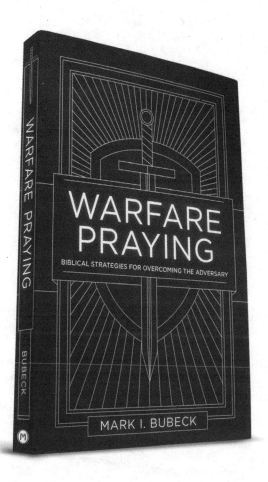

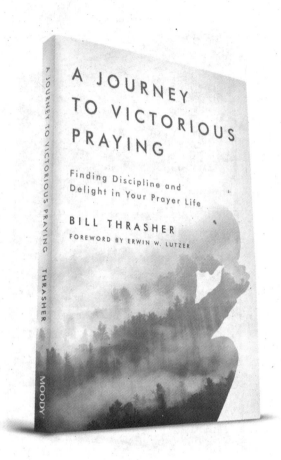